13

~ the Terrace

I was

minski

Blandford

CHILDREN'S
Names and
Horoscopes

CHILDREN'S
Names and
Horoscopes

Katharine Wyatt and Lesley Burrow

with Horoscopes by
Roger Elliot

EBURY PRESS
LONDON

Published by Ebury Press
National Magazine House
72 Broadwick Street
London W1V 2BP

First impression 1980

ISBN 0 85223 181 4

Produced by Granta Editions Ltd in association with
Book Production Consultants, 7 Brooklands Avenue, Cambridge

Designed by Tim McPhee

Printed and bound in Spain
Deposito Legal B –21272– 1980

Contents

ACKNOWLEDGEMENTS

Granta Editions wish to express sincere thanks to Miss Bay Robinson for agreeing to many illustrations by her father, Charles Robinson (1870-1937), appearing in this book. Granta Editions also acknowledge the help given by Mr. Geoffrey Robinson and the publishers of the following books, from which the Charles Robinson illustrations have been taken.

The Big Book of Nursery Rhymes Blackie 1903
pp.4, 6, 7, 8, 9, 14, 16, 34, 52, 56, 61, 79, 85, 90, 98, 99, 102, 128, 129, 139, 140, 141, 142, 146, 147, 148, 150 and 151. *Borders* pp. 6 and 7, 102, 130-138, 140 and 141.

The Big Book of Fables Blackie 1912
pp.57 and 143.

The Child World Bodley Head 1896
p.103.

The Cloud Kingdom Bodley Head 1905
Borders pp.104, 106, 108, 110, 112, 114, 116, 118, 120, 122, 124 and 126.

A Child's Garden of Verses Bodley Head 1895
Half title and p.144.

Lilliput Lyrics Bodley Head 1898
Back cover and frontispiece.

Alice's Adventures in Wonderland Cassell 1907
p.5 *Borders* pp.10-56, 58-101 and 144-151

True Annals of Fairyland: The Reign of King Herla Dent 1900
Title page

The Sensitive Plant Heinemann 1911
Front cover.

The 12 full colour illustrations appearing in *Signs of the Zodiac* and the black and white illustration for *The Family Tree* were drawn by Brian Warwick.

INTRODUCTION

This book offers a wide choice of names to help you select 'the right one' for your baby. We have included all the better-known names as well as many unusual but attractive ones; the latter may not have been used for some years, but will no doubt regain popularity with time. Many favourite names share the same etymological origin and may therefore be grouped together; if you like a particular name, you should also read through all its variations and diminutives — you may be surprised to find some very dissimilar names sharing the same root. The names and diminutives (in italics) have been placed in alphabetical order, not according to popularity.

As you will see from the descriptions, many names were invented by ancient civilizations or are derived from their languages; more recently, plant and flower names as well as virtues have been used. So if you wish to give your child an original name, don't be afraid to do so: others have in the past, which is why we have so many attractive names to choose from now. However, do call your baby something which sounds like a Christian name and is not so unusual that it will cause embarrassment later on in life.

The book continues with a horoscope section written by Roger Elliot and introduced on page 102. The final part deals with the practical issues a new-born baby presents, and we hope it will help you plan the equipment most suited to your purse and lifestyle. The Record section, with space for notes on two children, will provide you with a pleasing and practical reminder of your baby's characteristics at birth and of his or her progress in the first few months. It will also help you keep a useful record of vaccinations and childhood illnesses.

Katharine Wyatt and Lesley Burrow

Girls' names

A

Abigail: *Abbey, Abbie, Abby, Gail, Gayle*
This means 'father's joy' in Hebrew. An understanding and attractive woman of this name married to Nabal and later to King David is mentioned in the Bible. A popular name by the seventeenth century, it then came to mean a personal attendant and lost its appeal. Recently it has returned to fashion.

Ada: *Adda, Aida*
This name was introduced from Germany in the eighteenth century and became well known by the next century. Although less common now, it is sometimes used as the diminutive of Adelaide. The equivalent name in Old English meant 'prosperous' or 'happy'.

Adela: *Adele*
Brought to England by the Normans, Adela was originally German, meaning 'noble'. It was little used until the nineteenth century.

Adelaide: *Ada, Addy*
This is the modern French version of an old German name meaning 'noble sort'. It was widely used in the last century, often in a shortened form.

Adeline
This name developed from the same German origin as Adelaide and was introduced into England by the Normans. It was popular in the Middle Ages as Adelin and Edelin, and became fashionable again in the nineteenth century.

Adriana: *Adrienne*
Latin for 'woman of the Adriatic', Adriana is an unusual name. Shakespeare used it for one of his characters in *The Comedy of Errors*.

Agatha: *Aggie*
Originally from Greek, meaning 'good', this name was widely used in the thirteenth and fourteenth centuries. Agatha was the name of a third-century Sicilian martyr.

Agnes: *Aggie, Aggy*
Greek for 'pure' and 'chaste' or 'the lamb', Agnes was the name of a third-century virgin martyr who became the object of rites by unmarried girls. From the twelfth century it became more and more common, until by the sixteenth century it was one of the three most popular girls' names. After this its use diminished until it was revived in the eighteen hundreds.

Aileen: *Eileen*
This is an Irish name, equivalent either to Helen (bright one) or to Evelyn. It became well known in this country at the beginning of this century.

Ailie
This is the Scottish abbreviation of Alison.

Ailsa: *Ailssa*
A Scottish diminutive of Elsa. There is a similar name, Ailssa, originating from the Old German for 'girl of good cheer'.

Alana: *Alina, Allana, Lana*
Celtic, meaning 'beautiful' or 'fair'. This is the female version of Alan, and today it is a name that is growing in popularity.

Alberta: *Albertine*
A feminine form of Albert, which means 'noble and bright'. This name was sometimes used in the nineteenth century when Queen Victoria was on the throne and the name Albert enjoyed great popularity.

Albinia: *Albina*
From Latin, meaning 'white', this was the name of a third-century saint. It was first used in this country at the beginning of the seventeenth century and has been kept as a family name since then. The name is better known in Italy.

Alda
This is Old German for 'old' or 'rich'.

Aldora: *Alda, Dora*
There are two different meanings given to the name Aldora, the more common being 'winged gift'. However, another source suggests that it may mean 'being of superior rank'.

Aleris: *Aleras, Allerie, Ally*
Another unusual name, Aleris is of Greek origin and means 'belonging to a town near the sea'.

Alethea: *Alatea, Alitha, Althea*
From the Greek for 'truth'. This name came into fashion in the seventeenth century as a result of the courtship of Charles I with the Spanish infanta Maria Aletea and has been used occasionally since then.

Alexandra
In Britain this name was originally a Latinisation of Alexander that was used as a girl's name. More recently the name was made popular by the marriage of Edward VII (when Prince of Wales) to Princess Alexandra of Denmark.

Alexia
This name has been used as a diminutive of Alexandra and also as an alternative form of Alicia. However, it is a name in its own right and comes from the Greek for 'assistant' or 'helper'. Alexia is more widespread in East Europe, but in recent years has begun to gain in popularity in this country.

Alice: *Alicia, Ally, Alys, Alysia*
This name developed from Old French for 'noble and kind'. By the

twelfth century it was widely used as Alesia or Alicia. It was later thought of as old fashioned and was not revived again until romance writers used it in the nineteenth century. The publication of Lewis Carroll's *Alice's Adventures in Wonderland* further added to its popularity and it is widely used now.

Aline: *Adeline, Alina*
These names probably developed from Adeline and were common from the twelfth to the fifteenth centuries.

Alison: *Ali, Allie, Ally*
Alison was originally a French diminutive of Alice, which later became a name in its own right. It is a popular name now, especially in Scotland.

Alix
Alicia was the basis from which the name developed although phonetically it seems to have more in common with Alexandra.

Alodie: *Alodi*
A most unusual name, which almost sounds musical. Alodie in fact is Old English in origin and means 'wealthy'.

Alvina: *Vina*
This is the female form of Alvin. The meaning is of course the same, 'elf friend' or 'noble friend'.

Amabel: *Mabel*
From the Latin for 'lovable', Amabel was used in the twelfth and thirteenth centuries and soon became abbreviated to Mabel. It was later revived in the nineteenth century.

Amanda: *Mandy*
Amanda, which means 'worthy of love', seems to have been invented by seventeenth-century novelists and it now enjoys great popularity.

Amber
This little-known name has been used recently in America and stems from the name of the precious stone.

Amelia: *Emily*
Originally this name came from Germany, and is thought to mean 'industrious one'. It was common in the eighteenth century and was frequently anglicised to Emily. Both names are now used.

Amy
From the French 'to love', the name Amy was used occasionally in Britain from the twelfth century onwards. It was popularised in nineteenth-century novels and is now well known.

Anastasia
This comes from the Greek for 'she who arises' or 'resurrection', and was the name of a fourth-century saint. It has been used from time to time in Britain since the thirteenth century, but has been more commonly used in Ireland.

Anatola
Another name of Greek origin, Anatola is the feminine of Anatole. It means 'from the East'.

Andrea: *Andrina*
Andrea derived from the boy's name Andrew. As a distinct girl's name it was first used in the seventeenth century. Being the feminine of Andrew, the meaning of Andrea is 'womanly'.

Angela: *Angelica, Angelina, Angie*
From the Greek for 'messenger', the word originally referred to the celestial beings. As a Christian name it was sometimes used in Italy and France after the sixteenth century, but did not become popular in Britain until the end of the last century. It is now very well known.

Ann: *Anna, Anne, Annette, Annie, Anita, Nancy, Nanette*
This name, which derives from the Hebrew name Hannah, meaning 'grace', and which reputedly was that of the Virgin's mother, was introduced at the beginning of the thirteenth century. By the beginning of the seventeenth century it was one of the most frequently used names in this country. There have always been variations in the spelling, and Annette and Anita are respectively the French and Spanish versions.

Annabel: *Annabella*
Annabel, which has only been used quite recently in this country, is an old name that is probably the Scottish form of Amabel.

Anona: *Annona*
The Roman goddess of crops was called Annona. Hence the meaning of this somewhat unusual name is 'yearly crops'.

Anthea
From the Greek for 'flowery', Anthea was first used by poets in the seventeenth century and children have been christened with it occasionally since that time.

Antonia: *Antoinette, Antonina, Nina, Toni*
In the last two centuries these Italian and French versions of Antony have been used intermittently. Antonina, which is similar, was the name of a third-century Portuguese saint. Nowadays the diminutives Toni and Nina are quite common.

April: *Avril*
This name, which has only been used recently, comes from the name of the month. It sometimes has the French spelling Avril.

Arabella: *Ara, Arabelle, Bella, Belle*
The meaning of this name is uncertain but sources suggest it is Latin for either 'from Arabia' or 'beautiful altar'.

Ariadne: *Ariane, Arianna*
Although more popular in Italy and France, this name has of late been used in this country. It comes from the Greek for 'very holy one'.

Arminel
This is a little-known Devon name that is probably the English version of the French 'Armand'. It came originally from the German for 'army man'.

Astrid
Meaning 'divine strength' in Old German, this is a Norwegian name that has been taken up in this country very recently.

Athene
Athene, the Greek goddess of wisdom, the arts and handicrafts, was the daughter of Zeus. Her name, although rare, has been given to baby girls occasionally this century.

Audrey: *Audry*
A name that is quite popular now, Audrey evolved from the clumsy Old English name Etheldreda, which means 'noble might'. In the sixteenth century the word 'tawdry' arose from the cheap goods sold at St Audrey's fair, and consequently, because of the association, only the poorer classes used the name for a time.

Augusta: *Gus, Gussie*
From the Latin for 'venerable', Augusta was brought to England by way of Germany and became popular in the nineteenth century. Originally 'Augustus' was a title of honour first bestowed on Gaius Julius Octavianus, who was the adopted son of Julius Caesar.

Aurelia: *Auriol*
Aurelie was an eleventh-century French saint, whose name has continued to be regularly bestowed on girls in that country. It was introduced into this country as Aurelia in the seventeenth century and has been used occasionally since then. The word for 'gold' in Latin was the basis of the name.

Aurora: *Aurore*
Aurora was the Roman goddess of the dawn. Her name has been used in Britain infrequently.

Aveline
This was the original Norman name, which later became anglicised as Eveline and Evelyn.

Averil
The name of a seventh-century Yorkshire saint, Averil is still used occasionally in that area. In Old English it meant 'battle of the wild boars'.

B

Barbara: *Babs*

The Greek for 'strange' or 'foreign' was the basis for this name. From the twelfth to the sixteenth century it enjoyed a certain popularity, recalling as it did Saint Barbara, one of the great virgin saints, whose powers were invoked against thunder and lightning. There followed a period when it was rarely used, until revived at the beginning of the twentieth century.

Beatrix: *Bea, Beatrice, Bee, Trixie*

'Bringer of joy', this was the name of a Roman saint. A fairly popular name for many years, the name then went out of fashion. It was revived at the end of the nineteenth century because of its current literary associations in Shakespeare's *Much Ado About Nothing* and Dante's *Beatrice Portinari*.

Belda: *Belle, Belldame*

This is a French name meaning 'lovely or beautiful woman'. It is not often heard in this country however.

Belinda: *Linda*

'Linda' in this name comes from the Old German for 'snake' and is associated with cleverness. It was always a literary name from its use in the Charlemagne Romances to Pope's use of the name in *The Rape of the Lock*. The name is quite often used nowadays with no literary connotations.

Belle: *Bell, Bella*

These are usually abbreviations of Isabel or Isabella.

Benita

This Spanish version of the name Benedicta, from the Latin meaning 'blessed', has recently been introduced into Britain by way of America.

Bernadette

The boy's name Bernard was the origin of this girl's name. It is an unusual name in Britain, although sometimes used by Catholics in recognition of Saint Bernadette of Lourdes.

Bernice: *Berenice*

From the Greek for 'bringer of victory', this name has been occasionally used in Britain since the Reformation as it is mentioned in the Bible.

Bertha

'Bright.' This originally Frankish name has been used infrequently in this country since the Norman Conquest. It was more popular in the nineteenth century.

Beryl

This is a modern Christian name, taken from that of a precious stone.

Bessie: *Beth, Betsy, Bette, Betty*
These are all diminutives of Elizabeth.

Bethia
From the Hebrew for 'worshipper of Jehovah'. Bethia has been used since the seventeenth century, particularly in Scotland.

Bettina: *Bettine*
Although recognised as a name in its own right, Bettina is said to have originated from Elizabeth, and means 'blessed'. It is a name that is becoming more popular of late.

Beverley: *Beverly*
'Ambitious' in Old English, this was first used as a boy's name at the end of the nineteenth century. In America it then became popular as a girl's name, and it is now used as such in this country.

Bianca
This is the Italian form of the French name Blanche and means 'white'.

Blanche: *Blanch*
This name came from France in the thirteenth century and has been used infrequently since then. It became more popular in the nine-teenth century.

Blodwen
A Welsh name meaning 'white flower'.

Bonnie
A modern English name meaning 'good one'. In more recent years, Bonnie has begun to increase in popularity.

Brenda
This name comes originally from Shetland, although in Ireland it is considered to be the feminine form of Brendan. It has been widely used for over a hundred years, perhaps as a result of Scott's use of it in his book *The Pirate*.

Bridget: *Biddy, Bride, Bridie*
'The High One.' Bridget developed from the name of a Celtic fire goddess. It was not used as a Christian name in this country until the beginning of the sixteenth century and not until even later in Ireland, where it is now one of the most frequently used names.

Bronwen
A popular Welsh name, Bronwen means 'white breast'.

C

Camilla

In Virgil's *Aeneid* the queen of the Volski, Camilla, was killed by Aeneas' followers. The name was well known for a time after the publication of Fanny Burney's novel *Camilla* in 1796.

Candace: *Candice, Candy*

Since the seventeenth century this name has been used occasionally. It is mentioned both in Pliny and in the Bible. 'Glowing' or 'glittering white' is its meaning.

Candia

This is a Quaker name. It was taken from the place-name Candia (now Heraklion), the capital of Crete.

Candida

From the Latin, meaning 'white'. A saint of this name was said to have been cured by Saint Paul. Its use in England is very recent, perhaps since George Bernard Shaw's play *Candida*.

Cara: *Carina, Carine*

Cara is often heard as the diminutive of Caroline; however, it is an independent name that means 'friend' or 'beloved one'. It is sometimes heard in the form Carina.

Carissa: *Carl, Chrissa, Crissa*

Although a pretty name, Carissa means 'artful or skilful woman'.

Carlotta: *Carla, Carly*

These modern girls' names have developed from the German 'Karl' (Charles in English). Their meaning is 'woman' or 'strong'.

Carmel

In Hebrew this means 'garden'. It is the name of a mountain in Israel where there is a convent and church dedicated to the Virgin Mary, who was said to have frequented the area with Jesus when he was a child. The name is often used by Catholics.

Carmen

This is the Spanish for Carmel. This name has become better known recently with the boom in holidays to Spain.

Carol: *Carole*

This is probably an abbreviated form of Caroline. It is very popular in the Southern States of America. The name is now widely used in Britain, and sometimes given to girls born near Christmas because of Christmas carols. However, the meaning of the name is 'womanly'.

Carola

This is another name originating from Charles. It has never been particularly fashionable.

Caroline: *Caro, Carol, Carolyn, Carrie, Lina*
In Italian, Carolina was the girl's form of Carlo (Charles). It came to be used in Germany and was then brought to this country by George II's queen, Caroline of Bradenburg-Anspach. In the eighteenth century it was a popular name, as it is now. As with Carol, it means 'womanly'.

Cassandra
This is a Greek name. In tales of the Trojan War, Cassandra, the daughter of Priam and Hecuba, foresaw disastrous occurrences. It was a popular name in the thirteenth and fourteenth centuries and has been in use, if infrequently, since then.

Catharine: *see* Katharine

Catriona
This is a Gaelic diminutive of Katharine.

Cecilia: *Cecile, Cecily, Cicely, Ciss, Cissy, Sis, Sisley*
The Latin for 'blind' was the origin of this name. Saint Cecilia is the patron saint of music. A daughter of William the Conqueror was called Cecilia, and this made the name immediately popular at the time of its introduction.

Celeste: *Celestine*
From the Latin for 'heavenly'. It is more popular in France.

Celia
This name probably developed from Cecilia. It has been used as a Christian name in its own right since Shakespeare's use of it in *As You Like It*.

Charis
This came from the Greek for 'grace'. This name was introduced at the time of the Reformation and has been used occasionally since that time.

Charlotte: *Charleen, Charlie, Charline, Lottie, Lotty*
This is the feminine form of Charles, and means 'a man'. It was common in Europe before it reached England in the seventeenth century. It has remained popular since then, and at present is particularly in vogue.

Charmaine: *Charmain, Charmian*
This uncommon name is of Latin origin and means 'a singer'. It was popular in the 1920's after a song of the same name.

Cheryl
A modern name developed from the French for 'darling'.

Chloe
A Corinthian woman of this name is mentioned by Saint Paul in the New Testament. It was first used in Britain in the seventeenth century and has been bestowed on girls from time to time since then. It derives from the Greek for 'a budding plant'.

Chloris
An unusual Christian name used by seventeenth-century poets, Chloris comes from the Greek for 'blooming'.

Christabel: *Chris, Chrissy, Christy*
From the Latin for 'handsome anointed one', this name, although not common, has existed in this country since the Middle Ages.

Christian: *Christiana, Kirsty*
As the name suggests, it means 'a follower of Christ' in Latin. Although it has been around as a first name since the thirteenth century it has never been a favourite. It is probably more common today as a boy's name.

Christine: *Chris, Christina, Tina*
'A Christian' was also the origin of this name, which has been in existence since the time of the Norman invasion but has only recently become fashionable.

Cindy
This is a variation of the name Lucy.

Clare: *Clair, Clara*
This name, which means 'bright' and 'clear', spread to Britain from France in the thirteenth century. There were two French saints of that name, and also Saint Clare of Assisi in the thirteenth century, a friend of Saint Francis. She was the foundress of the order of Poor Clares, the second order of Franciscans. The Latinised Clara became fashionable in the last century.

Clarinda: *Clorinda*
Seventeenth- and eighteenth-century writers were fond of using this name, which is derived from Clare.

Clarissa: *Clarice*
These names were derived from Clare, as was Clarinda, and have been used for many years.

Claudia
This Roman name, meaning 'lame' in Latin, appears in the Bible. It was first used in Lancashire.

Clementina: *Clementine, Tina*
These girls' names developed from the boy's name Clement, which means 'merciful'. Clementine is probably better known as the heroine of the song now, although it was a popular name in the last century.

Cleo: *Cleopatra*
Cleo is a well-known modern abbreviation of Cleopatra, which comes from the Greek for 'glory' or 'fame'. There were seven queens of Egypt with this name, the most famous being Cleopatra VII, who was mistress to Julius Caesar and later to Antony.

Clodagh
This is an Irish name taken from the name of a river in Tipperary.

Clover
This flower name is a recent innovation.

Colette
In Britain, Colette, which originated from the French name Nicolette, has been used from time to time for many centuries. More recently it has been associated with a famous French novelist who wrote under that name.

Colleen
Colleen is an attractive Irish name meaning 'maiden'. It is not often heard in this country.

Constance: *Conn, Connie, Constantia*
A daughter of William the Conqueror was called Constance and it was with her that the name was introduced into this country, where it remained popular. The diminutive Connie is better known now.

Consuelo
This is an unusual name that comes from the Spanish for 'counsel'.

Cora
From the Greek for 'a young girl', this name has been used for less than a century and predominantly in America.

Coral
This name has only recently been used and calls to mind the precious material used in jewellery.

Coralie
Coralie is a French name invented after the Revolution, and sometimes used in this country.

Cordelia: *Delia, Della*
An unusual name that Shakespeare used in *King Lear*. It means 'jewel of the sea'.

Corinna: *Corin, Corinne*
From the Greek for 'a maiden', Corinna was a name coined by poets in the seventeenth and eighteenth centuries that has continued to be used from time to time. Corinne is the French version.

Cornelia: *Nela, Nelia, Nell, Nellie, Nelly*
Latin for 'horn coloured' or 'yellow'. In Greek mythology the cornel tree was sacred to Apollo.

Crystal: *Chrystal*
This comes from the name of the jewel. Chrystal is a Scottish variation of Christopher.

Cynthia
This is a name that has existed for a long time but did not become popular until the turn of this century. Cynthia, meaning 'from Mount Cynthus', was another name for Artemis (Diana), the goddess of chastity and hunting.

D

Dacia: *Dachia, Dachy*

This name means 'from Dacia', which was an ancient Eastern European country. It is rarely used as a Christian name.

Dagmar

A Danish name meaning 'joy of the Danes'. It has become more popular here in recent years but is still fairly unusual.

Daisy

This was originally a pet name for Margaret in Victorian times. In French the name Marguerite means 'daisy'.

Damaris: *Damara*

The Puritans adopted this New Testament name in the seventeenth century. In the Acts of the Apostles an Athenian woman of this name is mentioned as having been converted by Saint Paul. It means 'tame' or 'gentle'.

Danette: *Danny*

A feminine diminutive of Daniel, Danette means 'God has judged'.

Daniela

This is a modern girl's name derived from Daniel and has the same meaning as Danette. Of the two female versions, Daniela is more widely used.

Daphne

Greek for 'laurel'. Apollo loved a nymph of this name. She was later turned into a laurel bush. It has been used as a Christian name only in the twentieth century.

Davina

This is a Scottish feminine version of David that has been in use since the seventeenth century.

Dawn

A name not often used; it was invented this century.

Deborah: *Debbie, Debra*

This became a popular Christian name in the seventeenth century, when the Puritans adopted it. It comes from the Hebrew for 'bee'.

Dee

Rather a fashionable name, Dee means 'brunette beauty', and is a variation of Diana.

Deirdre

This name appears in 'Three Sorrowful Tales of Erinn', which has been the inspiration for many Irish poets and playwrights. It has been used as a Christian name only during the present century.

Delia: *Delena*

Eighteenth-century pastoral poets used this name frequently but its use as a Christian name is rare. It is derived from the Greek island Delos, birthplace of Artemis.

Delilah: *Lila, Lilah*
The story of Samson and Delilah is well known and a popular one in the Bible. It is no surprise that Delilah means 'the temptress'. It is not a common name at all.

Denise: *Denice, Denys*
Denis was a well-known girl's name from the twelfth century. The modern spelling is probably taken from the French, since the patron saint of France is Saint Denis.

Desdemona: *Desmona, Mona*
This name has been used occasionally since Shakespeare named the heroine of his famous tragedy *Othello* Desdemona. It means 'ill-starred' or 'sorrowful'.

Desirée
This unusual name has recently been borrowed from the French. It means 'desired'.

Devona: *Devina*
Either meaning 'brave' or 'from Devonshire'. It is not often heard at present.

Diana: *Di, Diane*
Diana is the Latin name of the moon goddess. It was fashionable in Renaissance times and has been used regularly since then. Diane is the French form of Diana and is now very popular.

Dillian
This unusual name probably derives from Old German.

Dilys
A modern Welsh name now quite common in this country, Dilys means 'genuine' or 'perfect'.

Dinah: *Dina*
From the Hebrew for 'judged', this was the name of one of Jacob's daughters.

Dione: *Dionetta*
A name of Greek origin meaning 'the daughter of heaven and earth'.

Dolores
In America this name is more popular than in Britain. It comes from the Spanish for 'pain' or 'grief'.

Dominick: *Dominica, Dominique*
The thirteenth-century Spaniard, Saint Domingo de Guzman, who founded the order of the Dominicans, gave rise to the popularity of this name, which comes from the Latin for 'the day of the Lord'. As Dominick, it was used both as a girl's and a boy's name for a while. Recently its use has become quite widespread.

Donella: *Donell, Nell*
A rare name meaning 'little girl'.

Donna

This is the more adult version of Donella and means 'refined lady'. It is a great deal more popular.

Dora: *Dorinda*

These are both names that have developed from Dorothy.

Doreen

Doreen is an Irish name in use since the beginning of this century. It is probably a derivative of Dorothy.

Doris

In the eighteenth century this name became suddenly popular and has been well known since then. It was the name of a sea nymph in Greek mythology, hence its meaning 'from the ocean'.

Dorothea: *Doff, Dolly, Dora, Dorothy*

From the Greek for 'God's gift', this name has been in an out of fashion for many years. Doll was a common diminutive until 1700, when it was first used for a child's plaything.

Dulcie

This is a modern name taken from the Latin for 'sweet'.

E

Eartha: *Ertha*

Eartha Kitt is probably responsible for making this most unusual name better known. Its meaning is 'the earth'.

Edith: *Eda, Ede*

Meaning 'rich', 'happy' and 'war', this is an Old English name which has never gone totally out of use.

Edna

This was first used in the nineteenth century. It appears several times in the Apocrypha and comes from the Hebrew for 'rejuvenation'.

Edwina

This is a modern feminine form of Edwin that comes from the Old English for 'happy friend'.

Eileen: *Aileen*

An Irish name, Eileen was taken up in England at the beginning of this century. It probably developed from Helen.

Elaine

As a Christian name this French version of Helen is not found until the nineteenth century after Tennyson used it in *Idylls of the King*.

Eleanor: *Eleanora, Elinor*

This was the Provençal variant of Helen, used in England since the time of Eleanor of Aquitaine, who was Henry II's wife.

Elfreda
Meaning 'elfin strength' in Old English, this was the name of the mother of Ethelred the Unready. The name fell into disuse after the Norman invasion but was taken up again in the nineteenth century.

Elizabeth: *Bessy, Beth, Betsey, Betty, Elisabeth, Eliza, Elsie, Libby, Liz, Lizzie, Lizzy,*
From the Hebrew for 'consecrated to God', this was the name of John the Baptist's mother. It was introduced into Britain from France in the thirteenth century but it was not until the time of Elizabeth I that it became one of the most popular names, a position it still maintains, perhaps aided by the fact that it is the name of the present queen.

Ella
This is a Norman name used for a couple of hundred years after the Norman invasion and then revived in the nineteenth century. It comes from the Old German for 'all'.

Ellen
A favourite name in Ireland, also in use in this country, which is an early English form of Helen.

Elma
A combination of Elizabeth and Mary led to the creation of this name, which is more common in America than here.

Eloisa: *Eloise, Heloise*
This is the modern Latinisation of Héloïse, a French name linked with that of Abelard in the unhappy love story. Meaning 'broad and healthy', its roots are in the Old German name Helewidis. Eloise is the more normal usuage these days.

Elsa: *Ailsa, Else*
Elsa is a name coming from the Old German for 'noble maiden' and should not be confused with Elsie, which is an abbreviation of Elizabeth. The Scottish form, Ailsa, is gaining in popularity in this country.

Elvira
This is a Spanish name that may possibly have developed from the German name Alverat. It means 'white' or 'blond'.

Emily: *Emilia, Emmy*
The name Emilia came into use in the eighteenth century. George II's daughter Emilia was known as Emily and this came to be used as a separate name as a result. Being the female forms of Emil, they mean 'industrious' or hardworking'.

Emma: *Emmeline*
Meaning 'universal one', Emma came to Britain from Normandy at the beginning of the eleventh century. It became particularly well known in the eighteenth century and is fashionable again now. Emmeline was the diminutive, which was common in the Middle Ages.

Ena

This was a popular name at the turn of the twentieth century because of Princess Victoria Ena, the granddaughter of Queen Victoria who later became Queen of Spain. It means 'ardent' or 'fiery one'.

Enid

A Welsh name meaning 'chaste', Enid has been used in this country for the past hundred years.

Erica

A modern girl's name from Eric, meaning 'ruler'.

Esme

Meaning 'loved one' in French, Esme was first used in Scotland and later spread across the border.

Esmeralda

This little-known name, which is used more frequently in literature than in real life, is taken from the Spanish for 'emerald'.

Esther: *Etty, Hetty, Tessa*

Persian for 'myrtle', this name exists in the Old Testament but does not appear as an English Christian name until the seventeenth century. It has been used occasionally since then.

Ethel

Originally this was a diminutive of names like Ethelfleda, Ethelburga and Ethelinda, in which 'ethel' is Old English for 'noble'. It became an independent name in the nineteenth century.

Eugenia: *Eugenie, Gene*

From the Greek for 'well born' or 'noble', this name was sometimes used in Britain from the thirteenth century. Napoleon III's wife was called Eugenie and this made the name more popular.

Eunice

This is one of the many names culled from the Bible in the seventeenth century, where it is mentioned as the name of Timothy's mother. It comes from the Greek for 'happy victory'.

Euphemia: *Effie, Phemie*

Mostly a Scottish name now, Euphemia comes from the Greek for 'pleasant speech'. The diminutive Effie is sometimes used as a separate name.

Eva: *Eve*

In the Book of Genesis, Eve is the name of the first woman, created by God to be the wife of Adam. In Hebrew it signifies 'living'.

Evadne

Greek for 'well tamed', a woman of this name, wife to Capaneus, threw herself on her husband's funeral pyre.

Eveleen: *Evelina, Eveline, Evelyn*

Eveleen is an Irish diminutive of Eve. Eveline is the anglicised version. At present the most common spelling is Evelyn.

F

Fabia
From the Latin for 'a grower of beans'.

Faith: *Fay*
This virtuous name was popular with the Puritans and is still fairly well known. Fay is a modern usage.

Felicity: *Felicia*
A name used since the twelfth century, Felicia was often confused with Phyllis. It comes from the Latin for 'happiness', as does Felicity. These are feminine forms of Felix.

Fenella: *Finola*
In Gaelic this means 'white shoulder'. The Irish spell the name Finola.

Fiona
From the Gaelic for 'fair maiden', this name was first used at the end of the last century.

Flavia
Flavia means 'yellow' in Latin.

Fleur
French for 'flower', this name has been popularised by Galsworthy's *The Forsyth Saga*.

Flora
Flora has been a common name in Scotland, where it was taken from the French at the time of the Renaissance. It was the name of the Roman goddess of flowers and gardens and more recently was that of the famous Jacobite heroine, Flora MacDonald.

Florence: *Flo, Florrie, Flossie*
In Latin this means 'blooming' or 'flourishing'. As a girl's name it has existed since the Middle Ages. The famous British pioneer nurse, Florence Nightingale, who was in fact named after the city in Italy where she was born, led to the great popularity of the name in the nineteenth century.

Frances: *Fanny, Francesca, Francie, Francis, Frankie*
Meaning 'from France', this name became popular in the Elizabethan period, although it had existed much earlier. Lady Jane Grey's mother was called Lady Francis Brendon. Francis is quite popular now. Francesca is the Italian version.

Freda
A Welsh name and diminutive of Winifred.

Frederica
In the nineteenth century this girl's name, which is derived from Frederick, meaning 'peaceful ruler', came into being.

G

Gabrielle
Gabrielle is of Hebrew origin and means 'woman of God'.

Gaeonor: *Gaynor*
These names both developed from the Welsh name Guinevere.

Gail: *Gayle*
An American shortening of Abigail, which has only recently been used in this country. Gail was probably introduced by Americans billeted here during World War II.

Gay: *Gaye*
This is a modern name, meaning 'happy', that enjoyed only a brief period of popularity.

Gemma
From the Italian for 'gem', this name has only recently been used in Britain.

Genevieve
The patron saint of Paris is called by this French name. Saint Geneviève sustained the population when Attila the Hun threatened to attack Paris. The name means 'white wave'.

Georgiana: *Georgette, Georgia, Georgie, Georgina*
These are eighteenth-century derivatives of George and mean 'tiller of the soil'.

Geraldine: *Gerry, Jerry*
A girl's name based on Gerald, it means 'mighty spear'.

Gerda
Popular recently in Britain, Gerda is taken from the little girl in Hans Andersen's tale of *The Snow Queen*.

Germaine
Meaning 'a German', this is a feminine version of the Norman boy's name, German.

Gertrude: *Gertie*
From Old German and meaning 'strong spear', the name has existed in Britain since the Middle Ages. It became popular at the end of the nineteenth century.

Gilda: *Gilli*
'Servant of God' is the meaning of this Celtic name.

Gillian: *Jill, Jillian*
A girl's name from Julian that is fairly popular at present. It means 'downy' or 'youthful'. The diminutive Jill is sometimes used as an independent name.

Gina
A modern name taken from Georgina.

Gisela: *Giselda, Giselle*
This comes from the German for 'promise'.

Githa: *Gytha*
This is an old Norse name that is seldom used.

Gladys: *Gwladys*
Gladys is a Welsh name, probably the equivalent of Claudia. It was adopted in England towards the end of the last century and is now well known. Gwladys is the Welsh spelling.

Glenda
This is a modern American name that has become popular in Britain in recent years.

Glenna: *Glen, Glennie, Glennis, Glynis*
An American girl's name from Glenn. Glennis is known to mean 'from the valley' in Welsh.

Gloria
A name that has only been used this century, this is taken from the Latin for 'glory'.

Grace: *Gracie*
A pleasant attribute name popular in the last hundred years.

Greta
A Swedish contraction of Margaret that is used occasionally in this country.

Griselda: *Grizel*
From the German for 'grey battle girl' or possibly 'Christ's battle'. Chaucer used the name in *The Clerk's Tale* and it was after this that it began to be given as a Christian name. It is now more common in Scotland.

Guendolen: *Gwen, Gwenda, Gwendolen, Gwendoline, Gwendolyn*
A Welsh name in which 'Gwen' means 'white'. The wife of Merlin the sorcerer was called Guendolen. It has been given as a first name since the nineteenth century in England. Gwen and Gwenda are contractions that are sometimes used independently.

Guenevere: *Guinevere*
Guenevere was the name of Arthur's queen in the Arthurian Legends. She was unfaithful to Arthur in her love for Sir Lancelot. The name means 'fair lady'.

Gwyneth
This means 'blessed' in Welsh.

Gwynne
From the Celtic for 'white'.

H

Hannah
From the Hebrew for 'God has favoured me', this was the name of the prophet Samuel's mother. It is a popular name in Ireland. However, although it has been quite a well-known name since the Reformation, it is Anna, the Greek version of the name, that has been more common in Europe.

Harriet: *Harry, Hatty*
The boy's name Henri was adapted to Henriette in France and this name was introduced into Britain by Charles I's queen, Henriette Marie. English pronunciation led to the development of Harriet and children were frequently christened with it in the eighteenth and nineteenth centuries. It is one of the older names that today are increasing in popularity.

Hayley
An unusual name that has become popular in recent years.

Hazel
This name was taken from that of the tree and has been used since the end of the last century.

Heather
Another plant name introduced in the nineteenth century.

Hedda
The famous play *Hedda Gabler* by Ibsen has caused this name to become better known. It is Old German and means 'war' or 'strife'.

Heidi
An Austrian name well known because of the children's book of that name by Johanna Spyri.

Helen: *Helena*
From the Greek for 'the bright one', this name became well known because of Saint Helena, to whom many British churches are dedicated, particularly because she was reputed to be of British origin. The name in fact was more common in Wales than in England, where Ellen was the accepted form. Helen and Helena were both revived after the Renaissance and are both popular names now.

Helga
Norwegian for 'holy', this name has been more popular in Scandinavia and America than in Britain.

Henrietta: *Etta, Harriet, Hetty*
A French feminine version of Henri that comes from the German for 'ruler at home'.

Hermia
From the Greek name Hermes, who was a messenger from the Gods.

He was also the God of wealth, luck, sleep and roads, and the conductor of souls to Hades. Shakespeare apparently revived the name in *A Midsummer Night's Dream*.

Hermione
From the same root as Hermia, this was another name brought into use by Shakespeare and other contemporary writers.

Hester: *Hetty*
This was an alternative version of Esther, Esther being the more common of the two at present.

Hilary
Hilary is more commonly used now for girls, as it was in the twelfth and thirteenth centuries. Meaning 'cheerful' in Latin, this was the name of a fourth-century French saint who was Bishop of Poitiers renowned for his fight against the Arian heresy. It is less common as a boy's name.

Hilda
This is an Old English name meaning 'battle maid'. Saint Hilda was an Anglo-Saxon abbess who founded the monastery at Whitby — an area in which the name has never ceased to be popular.

Holly
A modern usage from the evergreen plant associated with Christmas.

Honor: *Honoria, Nora*
From the Latin for 'honour and reputation', various derivatives became popular after the Norman Conquest, the more common being Honor in England and Nora in Ireland.

Hope
A seventeenth-century innovation by the Puritans

Hortense: *Hortensia*
Meaning 'a gardener' in Latin, this is basically a French name that has sometimes been used in this country.

I

Ianthe: *Iantha*
Greek myth tells us that Ianthe was a sea-nymph and the daughter of Oceanus and Tethys. The name means 'violet-coloured flower'.

Ida: *Idalina, Idaline, Idelle*
Either meaning 'industrious' or 'happy', Ida was brought to England by the Normans, and until the fourteenth century was quite a popular girl's name. In Irish it has become Ita, and there is an Irish saint of this name. Ida regained popularity during the last century in this country and is still in use today.

Ilona
A name that comes from the Greek and means 'light'.

Imogen: *Imogene*
This name seems to have sprung up because of an error in spelling made by the printer when Shakespeare sent his manuscript of *Cymbeline* to be printed. It is thought that the name intended in the play was Innogen. However, Imogen has emerged as an unusual name said to mean either 'image' or 'girl'.

Ina: *Ines, Inez*
Meaning 'pure', these names are all variations of Agnes.

Ingaret: *Inaret*
Ingaret is another name that is a variation, this one of Anchoret. However, it is Ingaret that is the better known of the two names today. The meaning is 'greatly loved'.

Ingrid: *Inga*
Of Scandinavian origin, Ingrid has only relatively recently become popular in other parts of Europe. Ing features in Norse mythology as a god of fertility, prosperity and the land, who seems to have left his mark more in Sweden than anywhere else. He was considered to be a great hero.

Irene: *Rena, Rene, Renie*
From the Greek, meaning 'peace', Eirene was the goddess of peace. There are several saints of this name, although none of them are particularly well known. The shortened versions are all popular.

Iris
'Rainbow' is the meaning of this name, which has Greek origins, although today it is probably more associated with the beautiful flower of the same name. It is of course also the name given to the coloured part of the eye. It is only since the beginning of the twentieth century that Iris has become popular as a first name.

Irma: *Irmina*
A noble name meaning 'strong, honourable', Irma is returning in fashion as a girl's name.

Isabel: *Bel, Bella, Isa, Isabella, Isabelle, Isobel*
This is a variation of Elizabeth that first became popular in the French court and then appeared frequently in Spain and Scotland. It seems that Isabel and Elizabeth were interchangeable for a great number of years, and both names were used even by queens. In the thirteenth and fourteenth centuries Isabel was one of the most popular names. It is still an attractive and frequently used name today. Isa is a pet form of Isabel and is also a name in its own right, meaning 'iron-willed'.

Isadora: *Dora, Dory, Isidora, Issy*
Isadora Duncan has made this name popular. It means 'gift' and is of Greek origin. There were two saints called Isidore, one of whom is the patron saint of Madrid, and as a result the name is fairly popular in Spain today, both for boys and girls.

Isla
A Scottish name probably meaning 'coming from the isles'.

Ismay: *Isamaya, Ysmay*
A most unusual name of obscure origins, Ismay and Ismey have been found occasionally in Ireland and England. They might possibly be connected to Ismenia, but there is no evidence of this.

Ismena: *Ismenia*
The origins are uncertain but Ismena is thought to be Celtic. Its major use was probably to give rise to several surnames, of which the most common are Jesmond, Jessimond and Emeny.

Isolda: *Isolde*
Made popular in the Tristan romances, Isolda is Old German and means 'ice rule' or 'the fair one'. Although common in the Middle Ages, today it is rarely heard as a girl's name and is connected only with music and Wagner's opera *Tristan und Isolde*.

Ivy
This is a relatively modern name that came into being in the nineteenth century when it was the fashion to use flowers and trees as names.

J

Jacinth
Being the name of a precious stone, Jacinth means 'purple' and can also mean 'hyacinth'. It is of Greek origin. In this country, it was first heard of as a boy's name. Today it is not often used.

Jacoba: *Jacobina*
This is the feminine of Jacob, Hebrew in origin, and means 'the supplanter'. The only part of the British Isles it appears to be in use today is Scotland. It is not a common name.

Jacqueline: *Jackie, Jacquelina, Jacquetta, Jakolina, Jaquennete*
Like Jacoba, Jacqueline comes from the boys' names James or Jacob, and means 'the supplanter'. There are many different forms of the name, but the most common in this country is Jacqueline, which is frequently abbreviated to Jackie. It was first brought to Britain from France, where it remains equally as popular today as in this country.

Jane: *Janey, Janie, Jayne, Jinny*
Johanna is a Hebrew name that has given rise to a great variety of girls' names. They are all feminine forms of John and mean 'gracious gift of God'. Jane was not a common name in England for many years. One of the earliest Janes of importance was Jane Seymour, one of the wives of Henry VIII, mother of Edward VI. Since then it has been sometimes fashionable, sometimes not. Today it is a most popular name, often put with another name, e.g. Sarah Jane, Mary Jane.

Janet: *Jan, Janette, Janina, Janine*
From the same root as the previous entry, Janet originated from the French form Jeanette as a diminutive of Jane. Today it is very much a name in its own right.

Janice
Janice today is a very popular name originating from Johanna and meaning 'gracious gift of God'.

Jasmine: *Jasmina, Yasmin*
Another girl's name which is the name of a flower, Jasmine is of Persian origin. It is a beautifully delicate name and unfortunately not frequently used today.

Jean: *Jeanne, Jeannette, Jeannie, Jennet*
Jean is the Scottish form of Jane or Janet, although it is now equally popular in England and Scotland.

Jemima: *Jem, Jemmie, Mina*
In the Bible we learn that one of the three daughters of Job was called Jemima. Its meaning is 'a dove' and it is Hebrew in origin. It may possibly be the feminime form of James.

Jennifer: *Jen, Jenifer, Jennefer, Jennie, Jenny*
Surprisingly enough, it is only during the last few decades that Jennifer has become generally used in Britain. It is in fact a Cornish form of Guenevere, and for many years was not heard outside Cornwall. Guenevere was the name of King Arthur's wife and the meaning of the name is 'fair lady'. Today Jennifer is a popular name.

Jessica: *Jess, Jesse, Jessie, Jessy*
Jesse was the basis of the girl's name Jessica and means 'he beholds'. It is of Hebrew origin. The pet name Jessie is often used today as a name in its own right rather than a diminutive. Although Jessica is generally considered old fashioned it is gaining popularity in this country amongst the younger generation.

Jill: *Jillian, Jillie*
This name is coming into its own although really it is a derivative of Gillian.

Joan: *Joanie, Jonie*
This is the nearest of the feminine versions of John. By the sixteenth century it was such a common name in this country that it was considered vulgar, and Jane replaced it as a respectable popular name. Joan was known earlier than Jane, hence Jeanne d'Arc is known in Britain as Joan of Arc, not Jean or Jane.

Joanna: *Joanne, Johanna*
Another variation on the same theme as the previous entry, Johanna was at first the more common spelling of this name, being a Greek spelling of the Hebrew Johanan. The 'h' is often dropped by parents of today and both Joanna and Joanne are popular.

Jocelyn: *Jocelin, Joscelin, Joslyn, Lyn*
This was an early German name that is thought to mean 'a Goth'. In England several surnames have come from Jocelyn, the most common of which are Gosling, Joslin, Joscelyne. The name has until recently been considered a boy's name, although the modern Jocelyn and its various spellings are feminine.

Joletta
An attractive name coming from the Latin for 'a violet'.

Josephine: *Jo, Josefa, Josepha, Josie*
Josepha was originally the feminine of Joseph, and it was not until the days of Napoleon's Josephine that the longer version became popular. The meaning of the name is 'God shall add', and it is a French adaptation of the original Hebrew. Josephine, Josie and Jo are all widely used in Britain – Josepha is no longer common.

Joy
Simply meaning 'joy', this short, sweet name occurs quite often today.

Joyce
Joyce is generally considered to come from the seventh-century Breton saint of the same name. In the Middle Ages it was both masculine and feminine, but the boy's name eventually died out and the girl's name survived. Jocelyn may well be a diminutive of Joyce, but this is not certain.

Judith: *Jodie, Jody, Judy*
Meaning 'Jewish woman', Judith is a very old name that reached this country in the ninth century. However, it is only fairly recently that it has become a popular name for girls.

Julia: *Juliana, Julie, Julienne, Juliet, Julietta, Jill*
A variety of girls names all coming from the same origin, this being the Julii, a Roman family renowned for their long hair, hence the meaning 'hairy' or 'downy'. Julia and Juliet are both names featured in Shakespeare. There was a Saint Juliana. Today Julia, Julie, Juliet and Jill are all well-known girls' names.

June
June is one of three popular girls' names taken from months of the year, the others being April and May.

Justina: *Justine, Tina*
Meaning 'just', this is the girl's form of Justin. Although not very common, there was a saint by this name who became the patron saint of Padua.

K

Kama

A most unusual name, Kama is Sanskrit for 'wished for'.

Karen: *Kara, Karena*

This name belongs to the many Katharine variations and is in fact Danish. Meaning 'pure', it has come to Britain as a name in its own right, and is very popular.

Karla: *Carla, Carly*

This is an alternative way of spelling Carla and has the same meaning. They are both feminine versions of Carl.

Katharine: *Catharine, Catherine, Cathie, Cathleen, Cathy, Kate, Kath, Katherine, Kathie, Kathleen, Kathryn, Kathy, Katie, Katrina, Katrine, Katy, Kay, Kit, Kitty*

All these names come from the same root – the Greek work 'katharos', meaning 'pure', 'chaste' or 'tortured'. One of the earliest bearers of the name was Saint Katharine of Alexandria. A Christian, she was sentenced to death like so many others for her beliefs, but before she died she was tortured on a wheel. This then is the origin of our Catherine wheel, which gives us pleasure on Guy Fawkes night. Why the name is spelt differently is not clear. It is a name that has always been popular, although some spellings are more frequently used than others. There are, as can be seen from the long list, a large number of diminutives and derivatives. The Irish form of the name is Kathleen or Cathleen.

Kay

Kay is used as a diminutive of Katharine, but it may also be a quite separate name. It could be the Welsh version of Caius meaning 'praise' or 'rejoice'.

Kelly

Gaelic for 'warrior maid', Kelly is an unusual name that has become most popular over the last few years.

Kerry

An Irish name meaning 'dark', this name is not very common in this country.

Kezia: *Keziah*

This name was given to one of the daughters of Job. So far, it has not been popular in this country.

Kieren: *Kieron*

These are both Celtic names meaning 'black'.

Kim

'Ruler' is the meaning of this brief name, which is given today to both boys and girls.

Kirsten: *Kirstin, Kirsty, Kristin*
Meaning 'a Christian', Kirsten is the Scandinavian version of Christine, but has become popular in Britain.

Koren: *Korine*
Greek for 'a maiden' or 'young girl', Koren or Korine is seldom used in this country.

L

Lara: *Larah*
Latin in origin, Lara means 'famous', and is fairly popular at present.

Larine: *Laraine, Larena, Larina, Rina*
Another name coming from the Latin and meaning 'seagull'.

Laura: *Laurel, Lauren, Lauretta, Lora, Loralie, Lorette, Lorna, Lorinda, Lorrie*
Laura is thought to be a shortened version of Laurencia, which is the girl's form of Laurence. If this is so, then it probably means 'laurel' or 'bay tree'. A number of girls' names appear to be variations of Laura, and they are all popular today, as they were several centuries ago. In history the most famous bearer of the name was Lora, Petrarch's mistress, and he addressed a number of his sonnets to her.

Lavinia: *Vina, Vinia, Vinnie, Vinny*
Lavinia in ancient legend was the wife of Aeneas, and the town of Lavinium, which is near Rome, is said to have been named after her. It is a name that was popular during the Renaissance and then went out of favour until the eighteenth century.

Leanne: *Liana, Lianne*
A common name today, which is simply the combination of two girls' names – Lee and Ann.

Lee
Meaning 'field' or 'meadow', Lee is today a very fashionable name. It is of course also a surname.

Leila: *Leilah, Lela, Lila*
A name meaning 'dark' or 'dark-haired', Leila is of Persian origin and is the name of a popular heroine in Persian romance. It was probably brought into fashion in this country by Lord Byron, who used the name in one of his poems, but is now unusual.

Lena: *Lina*
Lena is a derivative of Helen but today it is used independently and not as a shortened version. It means 'light' and is of Greek origin.

Leona: *Lennie, Lenny, Leonie*
The female version of Leo, Leona means 'lion'. It is not frequently heard nowadays and was more popular in the past.

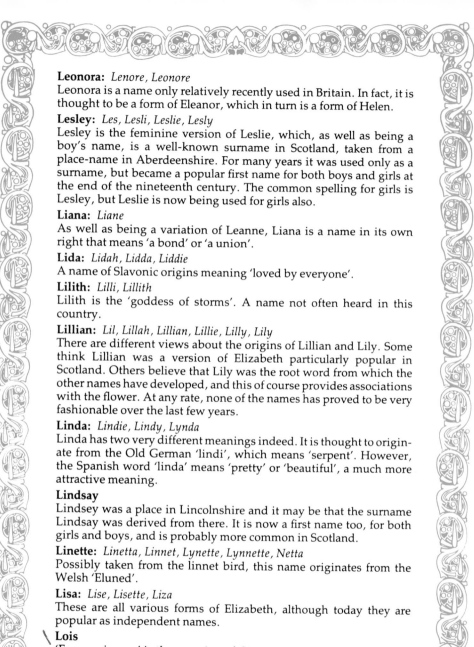

Leonora: *Lenore, Leonore*
Leonora is a name only relatively recently used in Britain. In fact, it is
thought to be a form of Eleanor, which in turn is a form of Helen.

Lesley: *Les, Lesli, Leslie, Lesly*
Lesley is the feminine version of Leslie, which, as well as being a
boy's name, is a well-known surname in Scotland, taken from a
place-name in Aberdeenshire. For many years it was used only as a
surname, but became a popular first name for both boys and girls at
the end of the nineteenth century. The common spelling for girls is
Lesley, but Leslie is now being used for girls also.

Liana: *Liane*
As well as being a variation of Leanne, Liana is a name in its own
right that means 'a bond' or 'a union'.

Lida: *Lidah, Lidda, Liddie*
A name of Slavonic origins meaning 'loved by everyone'.

Lilith: *Lilli, Lillith*
Lilith is the 'goddess of storms'. A name not often heard in this
country.

Lillian: *Lil, Lillah, Lillian, Lillie, Lilly, Lily*
There are different views about the origins of Lillian and Lily. Some
think Lillian was a version of Elizabeth particularly popular in
Scotland. Others believe that Lily was the root word from which the
other names have developed, and this of course provides associations
with the flower. At any rate, none of the names has proved to be very
fashionable over the last few years.

Linda: *Lindie, Lindy, Lynda*
Linda has two very different meanings indeed. It is thought to originate from the Old German 'lindi', which means 'serpent'. However,
the Spanish word 'linda' means 'pretty' or 'beautiful', a much more
attractive meaning.

Lindsay
Lindsey was a place in Lincolnshire and it may be that the surname
Lindsay was derived from there. It is now a first name too, for both
girls and boys, and is probably more common in Scotland.

Linette: *Linetta, Linnet, Lynette, Lynnette, Netta*
Possibly taken from the linnet bird, this name originates from the
Welsh 'Eluned'.

Lisa: *Lise, Lisette, Liza*
These are all various forms of Elizabeth, although today they are
popular as independent names.

Lois
'Famous in war' is the meaning of this name, which is the feminine
version of Louis.

Lola: *Loleta, Lolita*
Another diminutive that is used as a name in its own right, Lola is in

fact a shortened version of the Spanish name Dolores, or sometimes Carlotta. It has in recent years become quite popular in America.

Lorna: *Lorena*
Lorna Doone from the popular novel by R D Blackmore is the character who makes this name famous.

Lorraine: *Loraine*
'One who is famous in battle' is the meaning of Lorraine, which is a very popular name among this generation.

Louise: *Eloise, Lou, Louisa*
Louise and its variants is, is like Lois, the feminine of Louis and therefore has exactly the same meaning. Louise was not used in Britain until the seventeenth century but since then has always been very fashionable, along with Louisa. Lou is the pet form usually adopted.

Lucy: *Lucia, Lucile, Lucille, Lucinda, Lucretia*
Latin for 'light', is is interesting to learn that these names were in Roman times often given to children born at daybreak. In fact there was a Roman goddess Lucina who was the patroness of childbirth. Saint Lucia in the Middle Ages had her eyes put out before she was put to death and she thence became patron saint of people suffering from eye disorders. All forms of the name are very fashionable today.

Ludmilla: *Lovmilla, Mila*
Sounding very Russian, Ludmilla means 'loved by all'.

Lulu
A name popular today, Lulu is of Latin origin and means 'wolf'.

Luna
From the Latin for 'moon', it is not often used in this country.

Lydia: *Liddy, Lidia, Lydea*
Greek, meaning 'a lady coming from Lydia'. A name associated in the New Testament with Joseph's daughter, Lydia has survived through the generations and is still quite popular today.

Lyn: *Lynna, Lynne*
Originally a diminutive of either Madeline or Evelyn, Lyn and Lynne are particularly fashionable at present.

M

Mabel: *Belle, Mabella, Mabelle, Mable*
Mabel is a version of Amabel, and comes from the Latin word 'amabilis', meaning 'lovable'. It was very popular during the reign of Queen Victoria but today is not used so often.

Madeline: *Madalyn, Maddie, Madeleine, Madelena, Magda, Magdala, Magdalena, Magdalene*

Magdalene was the original name, and is taken from the birthplace of Saint Mary Magdalene, which was by the shore of the Sea of Galilee. She became the patron saint of penitents. The French version of the name is Madeleine, and in time this became Maudlin, which is in fact the pronunciation of the two famous university colleges, Magdalen College in Oxford and Magdalene College in Cambridge. Today it is the French name, Madeline, that is more popular as a girl's name in its various spellings. Occasionally Magda is heard, and this is the German abbreviation of the name.

Maida: *Maidena, Maidene, Maidy*

This uncommon name means 'maiden'.

Maire

Although Maire is the Irish form of Mary, it is a name used very frequently nowadays as a name in its own right.

Marah: *Mara*

A most unusual name, Marah is Hebrew for 'bitter'. Apparently it was the original Hebrew form of Mary.

Marcella: *Marcelle, Marcellina, Marcia, Marcy, Marsha*

These are feminine versions of Mark and mean 'belonging to Mars'. Marcie or Marcia are attractive variations that have become quite popular in recent years in America and to a lesser extent in Britain.

Margaret: *Daisy, Greta, Gretel, Madge, Maggie, Maisie, Margaretta, Margarita, Marguerite, Meg, Megan, Peg, Peggy*

Greek for 'a pearl', Margaret and its variants are of Persian origin. There was an early Saint Margaret of Antioch who was the patron saint of women in childbirth, but very little is known about her. A later saint of the same name was the wife or King Malcolm III of Scotland, and it was due to her that the name became so popular in Scotland. Margaret became widespread in England too, and in the Middle Ages was one of the most popular names of all. It is a name which has been used in most of the royal families in Europe at one time or another. Marguerite is one of the many variations and diminutives, and this, with Daisy, has associations with the flower of the same name.

Margery: *Marge, Margy, Marjorie*

These too are variations of Margaret, taken from the French Marguérite. Margery soon became considered as an independent name, with Marjorie being the Scottish spelling.

Margot: *Margo*

Margo also was adapted from Marguérite but has for a long time been used as a separate name.

Mari

A pretty name, with a sour meaning — 'bitterness'. Mari is one of the many different forms of Mary and is Irish.

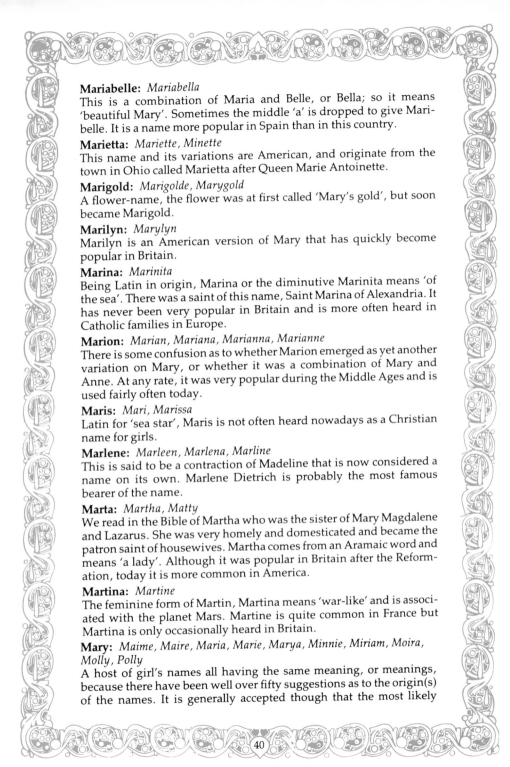

Mariabelle: *Mariabella*
This is a combination of Maria and Belle, or Bella; so it means 'beautiful Mary'. Sometimes the middle 'a' is dropped to give Maribelle. It is a name more popular in Spain than in this country.

Marietta: *Mariette, Minette*
This name and its variations are American, and originate from the town in Ohio called Marietta after Queen Marie Antoinette.

Marigold: *Marigolde, Marygold*
A flower-name, the flower was at first called 'Mary's gold', but soon became Marigold.

Marilyn: *Marylyn*
Marilyn is an American version of Mary that has quickly become popular in Britain.

Marina: *Marinita*
Being Latin in origin, Marina or the diminutive Marinita means 'of the sea'. There was a saint of this name, Saint Marina of Alexandria. It has never been very popular in Britain and is more often heard in Catholic families in Europe.

Marion: *Marian, Mariana, Marianna, Marianne*
There is some confusion as to whether Marion emerged as yet another variation on Mary, or whether it was a combination of Mary and Anne. At any rate, it was very popular during the Middle Ages and is used fairly often today.

Maris: *Mari, Marissa*
Latin for 'sea star', Maris is not often heard nowadays as a Christian name for girls.

Marlene: *Marleen, Marlena, Marline*
This is said to be a contraction of Madeline that is now considered a name on its own. Marlene Dietrich is probably the most famous bearer of the name.

Marta: *Martha, Matty*
We read in the Bible of Martha who was the sister of Mary Magdalene and Lazarus. She was very homely and domesticated and became the patron saint of housewives. Martha comes from an Aramaic word and means 'a lady'. Although it was popular in Britain after the Reformation, today it is more common in America.

Martina: *Martine*
The feminine form of Martin, Martina means 'war-like' and is associated with the planet Mars. Martine is quite common in France but Martina is only occasionally heard in Britain.

Mary: *Maime, Maire, Maria, Marie, Marya, Minnie, Miriam, Moira, Molly, Polly*
A host of girl's names all having the same meaning, or meanings, because there have been well over fifty suggestions as to the origin(s) of the names. It is generally accepted though that the most likely

meaning is 'bitterness'. The first known form of Mary to exist was Miriam, who was the sister of Moses and Aaron. However, it is the Virgin Mary, mother of Jesus Christ, who has always been greatly worshipped in Catholic communities, and is the better-known Mary in the Bible. It is interesting to learn that because the Virgin Mary was such a sacred figure, for a long long time nobody would have even considered naming their daughter after her. It was not until the twelth century that Mary began to gain popularity. There have been several Queen Marys, possible the most famous being Mary, Queen of Scots. Not long ago, Mary was one of the most popular names in this country. Today it is still used frequently, as are the various other forms – Maria is the Latin form used in Spain and Italy, Marie is French and Mamie American. Miriam, the original version, is Hebrew. The Irish versions are Maire or Moira. Minnie is Scottish, Molly and Polly are two of several terms of endearment coming from Mary.

Matilda: *Mathilda, Matty, Maud, Maude, Tilly*
Matilda is German and means 'great strength in battle'. Maud is the English version of the same name. Several surnames derive from Matilda, the most common of which are Madison, Mawson and Tilson. Today these Christian names are considered old fashioned.

Maureen: *Maurine, Mo*
Maureen is another name derived from Mary. It is Irish, and more closely connected with Maire, but is frequently used in this country as well as in Ireland.

Mavis
'The song thrush' is Mavis, a name once fairly popular but now dwindling and not often heard.

Maxine: *Maxime*
The feminine form of Maximilian, Maxine has the same meaning, 'the greatest'.

May: *Mae*
In its own right this name calls to mind the month in springtime. Otherwise it is yet another form of both Margaret and Mary.

Megan
A Welsh name meaning 'the strong', or possibly a derivation of Margaret.

Melanie: *Mel, Melania, Mellie, Melloney*
There were two saints called Melania, one grandmother to the other. Melanie is of Greek origin and means 'dark' or 'black'. It has in recent years become very popular in Britain.

Melinda: *Lindy, Malinda, Melina*
An unusual name of German origin.

Melissa: *Lisa, Mel, Melita, Melitta*
'Honey-bee' or just 'honey' is the meaning of this name, which

literature associates with a fairy. It is an old-fashioned name now making a comeback.

Melody
As the name suggests, Melody is connected with music. However, it is rarely heard as a girl's name.

Merle: *Meri, Meriel, Meryl*
Merle is 'the blackbird'.

Merry: *Merrie*
Merry means 'happy', 'mirthful', 'joyous'. It is of Old English origin.

Meta
Meta is another form of Margaret, although some sources say it comes from the Latin and means 'ambitious'.

Michelle: *Michaela*
This is the feminine form of Michael and is a French version. The meaning is 'being the image of God'.

Mildred: *Mil, Mildrid, Millie, Milly*
Old English in origin, Mildred means 'mild power'. There were three saints, all daughters of King Merowald, called Mildgyth, Mildthryth and Milburga, who were greatly worshipped during the Middle Ages. The name Mildrid or Mildred became very common in the nineteenth century but today is not at all fashionable.

Millicent: *Melesina, Millie, Milly*
Millicent sounds rather old-fashioned and is not in common use at present. It is German in origin and has the meaning 'energetic', 'one who works strongly'. One of the pet forms, Milly (shared with Mildred), reminds us of a favourite book for little girls called *Milly Molly Mandy*.

Mina: *Minna*
Although Mina is a shortened form of Wilhelmina it now exists as an independent name meaning 'memory'.

Mirabel: *Belle, Mirabelle*
'Wonderful' is said to be the meaning of this name, which is often shortened to Belle.

Miranda
Several names have been invented in literature. Miranda is one of these, the originator in this case being Shakespeare for his play *The Tempest*. It comes from a Latin word meaning 'worthy of admiration'.

Mona
Saint Mona was Irish and the name comes from the Irish word for 'noble'. This name has never been very popular in this country.

Monica: *Mona, Monique*
This, like the previous entry, is a saint's name, Saint Monica being best known as the mother of Saint Augustine. The name possibly comes from the Greek word 'monos', which means 'single' or 'alone', or the Latin word 'moneo', which means 'I advise'.

Morag
A name that is becoming fairly popular today, quite simply meaning 'the sun'.

Morna
An unusual girl's name meaning 'gentle' or 'beloved'.

Morwenna
'A wave of the sea' is a charming description of this name. There was a saint called Morwenna.

Muriel: *Meriel, Mur, Murielle*
Muriel was introduced to England by the Normans and it is a Celtic name connected with the sea. Once a popular name among the Jewish community, Muriel and Meriel are now not so common.

Myra: *Mira*
A name invented by the Elizabethan poet Fulke Greville, who introduced it in his love poems.

Myrtle: *Myrtilla*
This is the name of a shrub and has become a first name only during the last century.

N

Nadine: *Nada, Nadia*
Being Slavonic in origin, Nadine and its diminutives mean 'hope'.

Nancy: *Nan, Nanette, Nanny, Ninon*
These are all variations of Ann and Hannah.

Naomi
The story of Naomi is told in the Book of Ruth in the Bible and is a famous one. 'Pleasant' is the translation of Naomi, and we learn that because she has suffered greatly she says: 'Call me not Naomi, call me Mara (bitter): for the Almighty hath dealt very bitterly with me.'

Natalie: *Natala, Natalia, Natasha, Nathalie*
These names are all connected with Christmas and are often given to children born at this festive time of the year. Natalie and Natasha in particular have become popular names recently.

Nerissa: *Nerita*
Greek for 'of the sea'.

Nicola: *Nicole, Nicolette, Niki, Nikki*
These are feminine versions of Nicholas and have the same meaning, 'the people's victory'. Nicolette is not so common here as it is the French form; however, Nicola, Nicole and the shortened Nikki are all well known in Britain.

Nina: *Ninette*
Now occurring as individual names, both come from Anne — Nina is Russian and Ninette is French.

Nona: *Anona, Nonna*
Latin for 'the ninth', Nona is a rare name today. Perhaps the reason for this is that many families are not as large as they used to be, and there are not often as many as nine children for the ninth to be called 'Nona'.

Nora: *Norah, Noreen, Norine, Norleen, Norrie*
Nora comes originally from Honoria and is an Irish version. It is most popular as Nora, Norah and Noreen. Although Irish, it is often used in Britain.

Norma: *Normie*
This is the feminine form of Norman and seems to have appeared as a first name at the time of Bellini's opera *Norma* (1831).

O

Octavia: *Octave, Ottavia, Tavi*
The eighth child born to a family is Octavia, or Octavius for a boy.

Odette: *Odet, Odetta, Odila, Ottilia*
Odette is the French form of the name Ottilia, which comes from Old German and is translated to mean 'the fatherland'. There was a seventh-century saint called Ottilia, but neither names nor the derivatives are common in Britain at present.

Olga
'Holy' is the meaning of Olga, a Russian name that originated in Scandinavia. Saint Olga of Kiev is famous as she is thought to be the first Russian to be baptised into the Christian faith.

Olive: *Livia, Livvi, Livy, Olivia, Ollie*
Although Olive is possibly the more common name today, Olivia is thought to have existed first, as the girl's form of Oliver. The olive branch is the symbol of peace and Saint Oliva became the patron saint of olive trees. Her name day is in June during the time of the olive crop.

Olwen
Legend tells us of Olwen, a giant who had white trefoils spring up behind her wherever she went, hence the meaning of the name, 'white footprint'. It is a Welsh name.

Ophelia
Made famous by Shakespeare in his tragedy *Hamlet*, Ophelia is of Greek origin and means either 'serpent' or 'help'.

Oriana

An unusual name of Latin origin. The meaning is uncertain.

Oriel: *Oriole*

There are two possible origins of the name Oriel. It may well have come from the ornithological name of the golden thrush, or possibly from the Old German for 'strife', 'fire'. As a Christian name it is not well known. Oriel College Oxford is not connected.

P

Pamela: *Pam*

A name coming from the Greek and meaning 'all honey', Pamela is another example of a name invented for a literary figure. Sir Philip Sydney introduced it about 1580–1590 for a lady in his book *Arcadia*. However, it was a later writer, Samuel Richardson, who used it for the main character of his novel *Pamela*, who made the name popular. Today it is fairly fashionable.

Patience: *Patty*

A rather stern name, Patience, as expected, means 'patient' or 'long-suffering'. At one time it was used for both girls and boys. Today it has become very uncommon among the younger generation.

Patricia: *Paddy, Pat, Patsy, Pattie, Patty, Tric, Tricia*

The patron saint of Ireland is Saint Patrick, but strangely enough Patricia, the feminine form, was originally heard first in Scotland in the eighteenth century. Today, Patricia and its various derivatives are all popular throughout Britain. It is said to mean 'nobility' or 'well born'.

Paula: *Paulina, Pauline, Paulette, Pol*

Paula and Pauline are the most common of these names, all from the Latin root meaning 'small'. They are all feminine forms of Paul. As well as the very famous Saint Paul, there was a Saint Paulina in the fourth century who founded several convents in Bethlehem. Pauline and Paulette are both French versions, of which the former is more often heard in Britain. Paula is becoming increasingly fashionable.

Pearl: *Pearle, Perl, Perlie*

Like Ruby and Crystal, Pearl is a jewel that in recent years has become popular as a Christian name.

Penelope: *Pen, Penny*

The legend of Penelope whose husband Ulysses left her behind while fighting in the Trojan war for ten years is well known. The name means 'bobbin' or 'weaver'. The Irish form is said to be Fenella, and both names are attractive and fashionable.

Perdita

Now not in common usage, Perdita is based on the Latin for 'lost'. Shakespeare invented it for his play *A Winter's Tale*.

Petrina: *Petra, Petrine, Trina*

The feminine form of Peter, Petrina has the same meaning, 'steadfast', 'rock'.

Petula

This name is very modern and the meaning and origin are unknown.

Philippa: *Phil, Pippa*

Although Philippa has existed since the Middle Ages it is interesting to learn that for many years girls were actually called Philip. Today, Philippa and the pet-form Pippa are both popular. They mean 'lover of horses'.

Philomena: *Phil, Philomel*

This comes from a similar root to Philippa and means 'one who loves mankind'. Today it is not in common use.

Phoebe: *Phebe*

'Bright' or 'shining', Phoebe was one of the names the Greeks gave to the goddess of the moon. It was fairly popular during the seventeenth century in this country and today is occasionally heard.

Phyllis: *Phillida, Phillis, Phyl*

Greek legend tells of the maiden who killed herself for love and turned into an almond tree. Hence the meaning of the name, 'leafy' or 'a green branch'. At one time the name was tremendously popular and appeared frequently in poetry, usually associated with a country maiden. In recent years it has ceased to be so common.

Poppy

Not in common use, Poppy is a flower name.

Portia

Another name associated with Shakespeare, Portia is an Old Latin name meaning 'connected with pigs'.

Primrose: *Rose, Rosie*

Primrose, like Poppy, is a flower name that was popular during the eighteenth century.

Priscilla: *Cilla, Pris, Prissie, Prissy*

'Ancient' is the meaning of this Latin name, which appears in the New Testament. A modern shortened form is Cilla, which is quite popular today.

Prudence: *Pru, Prue*

'One who is discreet', Prudence is a first name like Faith and Hope that has survived, unlike Temperance or Obedience. They are all rather tall orders as names, especially for a young, lively child, and as a result seem to be dying out slowly.

Prunella

An attractive name with a dull meaning — 'plum-coloured'!

Q

Queenie: *Queena, Queeny*
This has developed as an independent name, although it originated as a pet form of Regina and, during the reign of Queen Victoria, of Victoria. Today it is sometimes used as term of endearment, but only occasionally.

R

Rachel: *Rachele, Rachelle, Rae, Ray*
Today a highly popular name, Rachel is Hebrew for 'a lamb' or 'an ewe'. It is a name that features early on in the Bible and for many years has been a common name for Jewish girls. Now it is frequently used amongst all races and creeds.

Ramona: *Mona*
An unusual name meaning 'protector', this is the female form of Raymond.

Rebecca: *Becky, Reba, Rebekah*
A Hebrew name that might mean 'heifer'. The wife of Isaac was called Rebecca, although it was spelt in the less common way Rebekah. It became very popular in the seventeenth century and today also is a favourite name.

Regina: *Gina, Regine*
Latin for 'queen', Regina is more common on the Continent than in Britain.

Renata: *René, Renée, Reni*
None of these names are English, although they are occasionally heard in this country. They come from the Latin, meaning 'born again', 'reborn'. Renata is German and René and Renée are French.

Rhoda: *Rhodah, Rodi, Rodie*
A flower name, Rhoda is Greek for 'rose'. It has been used as a first name only since the seventeenth century, although it is a name mentioned in the Bible.

Rhona: *Anna, Roanna, Rona*
This name is of uncertain origin. It is thought that Roanna means 'sweet', but very little is known about it. Rona may possibly be based on the boy's name Ronald and would therefore mean 'powerful judgement'.

Ricarda: *Rica, Richenda, Richenza*
These feminine forms of Richard mean 'ruler'. None of them are common in this country at present.

Rita: *Reta*
Rita is a diminutive of Margarita and has the same meaning, 'a pearl'. Today it is used as a separate name.

Roberta: *Bobbie, Bobby, Robenn, Robin, Robina*
The feminine form of Robert, this name means 'bright fame'. The variation Robin is increasing in popularity as a girl's name.

Rosa: *Rosabel, Rosabella, Rose, Rosetta, Rosie, Rosina*
'A rose' or 'beautiful rose', all these different forms are heard as first names today.

Rosalia: *Rosalie, Rozalia*
Although connected with Rosa, Rosalia is actually the name of an annual ceremony at which garlands of roses are hung on tombs. Saint Rosalia was the patron saint of Palermo and the name rapidly became popular throughout Italy and, later, France.

Rosalind: *Ros, Rosaleen, Rosalinde, Rosaline, Rosalyn, Roslyn*
There are two very different meanings for this group of names. The first, in connection with the names above, is taken from the Spanish words 'rosa' meaning 'rose' and 'linda' meaning 'pretty'. The other, somewhat opposed meaning comes from German words that mean 'horse-serpent'. Shakespeare's use of it in several plays made it very popular in Elizabethan times and it is still used, though to a lesser extent, today.

Rosamund: *Rosamond, Rosamunda*
Again, the German and Spanish origins give rise to two varying interpretations of this name: either 'horse protection' or, more attractively, 'pure rose'. A famous English Rosamund was the mistress of King Henry II, Rosamund Clifford, who was poisoned by the king's wife, Elinor. Rosamund is today one of the most frequently used of the 'Rose' names.

Rosanna: *Rosanne, Roseanna, Roseanne*
Rosanna and its variations are an example of two names combined to make one — Rose and Anna.

Rosemary: *Rosemari, Rosemarie*
This is a combination of Rose and Mary, although it is also the name of a plant. It was thought in olden days that the rosemary plant refreshed one's memory. Today it is a popular name and is occasionally spelt in the French way, Rosemarie.

Rowena
Thought to mean 'famed friend', Rowena found popularity after Sir Walter Scott had used it for the heroine in his novel *Ivanhoe*.

Ruby
'Red' is the meaning of this name, which is taken from that of the precious jewel. It is relatively modern as a Christian name but not very popular.

Rue
A Greek name taken from the plant called rue.

Ruth: *Ruthi, Ruthie*
A famous figure in the Old Testament, the name Ruth is thought to mean 'beauty' or possibly 'friend'. It came into use in Britain after the Reformation and was extremely popular during the seventeenth century but is not so common now.

S

Sabina: *Sabin, Sabine, Savina*
Latin for 'a Sabine man or woman', this being an ancient Italian tribe. It has survived as a woman's name only but is not common now.

Sabrina: *Brina*
This name may mean 'a princess' or be taken from the poetical name of the River Severn and mean 'a nymph haunting the Severn'.

Sadie: *Sadye*
Sadie is one of the forms of Sarah and is the American version.

Salena: *Sal, Sali, Salina*
Another unusual name, this one is said to mean 'salty'.

Sally: *Sal, Sallie*
Sally and Sallie were originally pet forms of Sara, but today they are used as independent names, with their shortened version Sal.

Samantha: *Sam, Sama, Sammie*
Samantha is a very modern name that seems to have originated in America and become very popular during the last ten years. It is not thought to have any connection with the boy's name Samuel. Very little appears to be known about how the name came into being; it may be an American Indian name meaning 'lovely flower' but this is not certain. However, it has proved to be one of the most fashionable names of recent years.

Sandra: *Sandie, Sandy*
This is in fact a diminutive form of Alexandra or the original Italian, Alessandra. However, today it has become a favourite as a name in its own right.

Sarah: *Sara, Sarene, Sarita*
The wife of Abraham was called Sarah and this Hebrew name means 'princess'. It became popular after the Reformation. Often the final 'h' is dropped to give Sara.

Selena: *Celina, Lina, Selene, Selina*
This name has obscure origins. It may come from the Greek word for 'moon' or more likely is derived from the French 'Céline', meaning 'heaven'.

Serena: *Serina, Sirena*
Very similar sounding to the name above, Serena comes from the Latin for 'tranquil', 'calm'. It is not a common name.

Sharon
Sharon and Sarene are names originating from Sarah.

Sheena
This is a name worth mentioning since it is heard fairly often today. It is simply the English pronunciation of Sine, which is Gaelic for Jane.

Sheila: *Sheelah, Shelley*
Although Sheila may be thought to be a name in its own right, like Sheena, it is a different way of pronouncing another name. This time it is the English way of saying 'Sile', which is Irish for Celia and means 'blind'. Today it is a popular name and often not connected at all with Celia or Cecilia.

Shimona
Hebrew for 'little princess', Shimona is an attractive name that is occasionally heard in this country.

Shirley: *Sheri, Sherry, Sheryl, Shirl, Shirlie*
The famous child actress Shirley Temple has caused the great popularity of this name. Originally Shirley was a surname, taken from a place-name, and popular in Yorkshire. It then seems to have been a boy's name, until Charlotte Brontë called the heroine of one of her novels Shirley. Sheryl and its forms are variations.

Sibyl: *Sib, Sibbie, Sybil*
A Sibyl in ancient Greece and also Rome was a woman who interpreted the wishes of the oracles. These oracles were called the sibylline oracles. Both Virgil and Livy refer to them in their works. The Normans introduced the name to England. It is now more common in the form Sybil.

Silvia: *Silva, Silvana, Syl, Sylvia, Sylvie*
Latin for 'wood' or 'wood dweller', Silvia or Sylvia came into vogue in Britain after Shakespeare used it for one of the heroines in *The Two Gentlemen of Verona*. The mother of Romulus and Remus was called Rhea Silvia and this caused the name to grow in popularity in Italy.

Simona: *Simone, Simonetta*
These are feminine forms of Simon and mean 'hearkening'. They are Hebrew in origin.

Sonia
The Russian form of Sophia is Sonia, with its various spellings, and is often heard today.

Sophia: *Sonia, Sonja, Sonya, Sophie, Sophy*
Saint Sophia had three children, called Faith, Hope and Charity. The name is Greek for wisdom and was a name often used in European royal families. In particular it was a favourite in Germany, and was

brought to this country by George I. At one time it seemed to go out of fashion, but today is one of the names fast coming into vogue.

Stella: *Estella, Estelle, Stel*
Latin for 'star', Stella became fashionable owing to the sixteenth-century poet Sir Philip Sidney and the originator of *Gulliver's Travels*, Jonathan Swift, using it in their literary works.

Stephanie: *Stefanie, Stephania, Stevie*
Stephen was the basis of these names, which mean 'garland' or 'crown'.

Susan: *Sue, Suki, Susana, Susannah, Susanne, Susie, Suzanne, Suzette, Suzie*
These names are taken from the Persian city Shushan, known as the City of White Lilies, from which we get the meaning 'lily'. Although it sounds quite a modern name, Susanna appears in the Bible and was first introduced to Britain in the Middle Ages. During the eighteenth century it reached its height of popularity and gradually, as time went by, the shortened form Susan became more frequently used. Today, in all its forms, it is still a very fashionable name.

T

Tabitha: *Tabbie, Tabby*
Tabitha is Aramaic for 'gazelle' or 'roe'. It is a Biblical name. Although it was fashionable two or three centuries ago it is not in common use today.

Tamara: *Tamar*
A Russian name coming originally from the Hebrew and probably meaning 'palm'. It is very unusual but becoming fashionable.

Tamsin
A feminine derivative of Thomas.

Tanya: *Tatiana*
Tanya is the abbreviated form of Tatiana, but much the more common name today. There was a famous martyr called Tatiana during the third century. The meaning is obscure, although it is believed that the name orginated in Asia. Tatiana is apparently fashionable in Russia and Tanya is growing in popularity in this country.

Tara
Celtic for 'a crag' or 'a tower', Tara is another unusual name that has become popular of late.

Teresa: *Terese, Terry, Tess, Tessa, Theresa, Therese, Tracy*
There are two islands called Therasia: one is near Sicily and the other near Crete. Some believe that the name came from these islands, meaning 'a woman from Therasia'. Others say that it means 'a har-

vester'. One of the earliest bearers of the name was Saint Therasia, who was Spanish and lived during the fifth century. Until the sixteenth century the name remained in Spain alone, when the fame of Saint Teresa of Avila spread it to the rest of the Roman Catholic world.

Thalia
Greek for 'blooming'.

Theodora: *Dora, Dori, Thea, Theda, Theo, Theodore*
This is the feminine form of Theodore, which means 'God's gift'. There were twenty-eight saints called Theodore but despite this the name did not become common in Britain until the nineteenth century. Theodora is rarely heard nowadays; perhaps Thea is more popular.

Theodosia
A name from the same root as the previous entry, Theodosia comes from the Greek, meaning 'divine gift'.

Thora
A name of Norwegian origin meaning 'thunder'.

Tiffany
Tiffany is the diminutive of Theophania and is used as a name in its own right. It means 'manifestation of God'.

Timothea: *Thea, Tim, Timmie*
'Respecting God' is the meaning of this name of Greek origin, which is of course the female form of Timothy. It is rarely heard as a girl's name today.

Tina
Tina has become so popular a pet form for girls names either Christina or Clementina that it is now often heard as an independent name.

Tracy
Based on the boy's name Thomas, meaning 'a twin', Tracy is a modern name.

Trina: *Tini, Treen, Trinia*
An unusual name that may be thought to be a diminutive form but is in fact an independent name, Trina is Greek and means 'pure'.

Topaza
This comes from the precious stone, the topaz, and is not in frequent use today.

U

Udele: *Uda*
'One of great wealth' is what this unusual Old English name means.

Una: *Ona*
Una is an Irish name taken from the Latin word 'unus', which means 'one'. The correct Irish spelling is Oonagh while another version of the name gives Juno. The English version of Una is Winifred or Winnie, but Una is used occasionally.

Undine
A name coming from the Latin for 'of water' or 'of the waves'.

Urania
Another uncommon name, Urania was used in literature by the sixteenth-century poet Sir Philip Sidney. It means 'heavenly'.

Ursula: *Ursa, Ursel, Ursie, Ursulette*
This is the diminutive of Ursa, which of course comes from the Latin for 'little she-bear'. There is a famous legend about Saint Ursula, who was shipwrecked along with 11,000 others. The Order of teaching nuns known as the Ursulines took their name from her. Today Ursula is more popular as a name than Ursa.

V

Valda: *Val*
An unusual name that is occasionally heard today, Valda means 'heroine of the battle' and is Old German in origin.

Valentina: *Valencia, Valentia, Valora*
The feminine form of Valentine, who was a Roman martyr-priest during the third century. He was martyred on 14 February, which was also the eve of the festival of Juno, at which time lots were drawn for lovers. This festival was changed to Valentine's day and is still celebrated throughout the world. Sometimes girls are called Valentine, but Valentina is the actual feminine version. It is not at all common but was made famous by the first space-woman, who was Russian and called Valentina Tereshkova.

Valerie: *Val, Valeria*
This popular name originated with a Roman family, the Valerian clan, which was highly honoured and distinguished. Valérie is the French version and the name was introduced to Britain through France. It has been used in this country for only about 100 years.

Valonia
As it may suggest, Valonia means 'a valley dweller' and is of Latin origin.

Vanessa: *Vanesa, Vanni*
A popular name invented by the eighteenth-century novelist Jonathan Swift and used ever since.

Varina
A Greek name meaning 'stranger'.

Velda: *Veleda*
'A wise woman', Velda is a German name sometimes used in this country.

Vera
Vera is sometimes confused with the name Veronica and said to mean 'true'. In fact it comes from the Russian word 'viera' meaning 'faith'. It has been a popular name in Russia for many generations but in Britain only since the beginning of the present century.

Verena: *Verinia*
Verena was a virgin martyred in Switzerland, to whom many churches have been dedicated in that country. It is not often heard in Britain.

Verity
Simply an abstract noun, it has been used as a first name for girls in this country since the seventeenth century. It is not so popular now as it once was.

Veronica: *Nicky, Ronnie*
Legend relates how a woman wiped Jesus's wounded face while he was carrying his cross to Calvary, and afterwards when she looked at her cloth she saw in it the image of the face of Jesus. She became known as Saint Veronica, as the Latin word 'veraiconica' means 'a true image', and was adopted as the patron saint of photographers. It is a name that was most popular in France and later used a certain amount in this country. It has never been very popular.

Victoria: *Vickie, Vicky, Victorie, Victorine*
The feminine form of Victor, Queen Victoria is the most notable bearer of the name. Surprisingly the name was for a long time more popular as a second name and it is only in recent years that it has become fashionable.

Viola: *Vi, Violet, Violetta*
This is a flower name more often heard as Violet. Symbolically it is associated with modesty, and with the heroine of Shakespeare's *Twelfth Night*.

Virginia: *Ginger, Ginny, Jinny, Virg, Virginie*
This name is usually associated with virgins and maidens but in fact it probably came from an old Roman family called Virginius. In America the name was connected with Queen Elizabeth, 'the Virgin Queen', and given to the first British child born in America after Sir Walter Raleigh had named Virginia after his queen. It is still more widely used in America than in Britain.

Vivian: *Vi, Viv, Vivien, Vivienne*

This is a name for both sexes; however, Vivian is more often the boy's form and Vivien the girl's spelling. Both are used for girls. The name is connected with 'life' and is usually said to mean 'lively' or 'animated'.

W

Wanda: *Wenda*

Wanda is a name that has been growing in popularity of late. It probably means 'the wanderer'.

Wendy

Another name connected with literature, Wendy was the name J M Barrie gave to the girl in his famous play *Peter Pan* and since then it has been in vogue. Occasionally it is used as a shortened form of the name Gwendolen.

Wilhelmina: *Mina*

This name is Old German and the feminine form of Wilhelm, which means 'helmet'. It is now rarely used in Britain.

Willa

This is one of the feminine forms of William.

Winifred: *Freda, Win, Winnie*

Saint Winifred was Welsh and the name means 'friend of peace'. She was beheaded for refusing to marry a prince in the first century. The name became popular in this country in the sixteenth century and has remained here ever since.

Winona: *Wenona*

An uncommon name that is thought to be of American-Indian origin meaning 'first-born daughter'.

Wynne

A Celtic name meaning 'fair' or 'white'.

X

Xena: *Xenia, Ximena*

A Greek name not often heard in this country, meaning 'one who is hospitable'.

Xylia

Another Greek name, meaning 'coming from the wood'.

Y

Yasmine
An alternative spelling of Jasmine, which is a flower name.

Yolande: *Yolanda, Yolanthe*
This is the French form of the flower name Violet. It is quite a common name, probably more fashionable than Violet.

Ysolde
'Fair one' is the meaning of this Celtic name.

Yvonne: *Ivonne, Vonnie, Yvette*
Yvonne and Yvette are French names that are quite popular in Britain. The meaning of the names is uncertain but may be 'yew tree'. One source suggests that it may originate in Scandinavia and mean 'archer'. Neither definition is certain.

Z

Zadia
'One of fair mind' is said to be what this Greek name means.

Zandra
Another spelling of Sandra, this is a feminine version of Alexander. It means 'friend' or 'helper of mankind'.

Zena: *Zenia*
Like Xena, Zena is also Greek and means 'one who is hospitable'.

Zenobia: *Zenovia*
'Father's ornament' is the meaning of this name. Zenobia was a martyr during the fourth century. Her name was at one time popular in the West Country.

Zillah
A Hebrew name meaning 'shade'.

Zoe
A third-century martyr was called Zoe. This name means 'life' and is Greek. Today it is becoming fairly popular.

Zora
A most unusual name coming from the Latin for 'dawn'.

Zuleika
A name sounding very Arabic, which in fact it is, Zuleika means 'fair'.

Boys' names

A

Aaron: *Aron, Aharon*
Aaron was the name of the first High Priest of Israel, the brother of Moses. It is an unusual but pleasant name whose obscure origins may be in either the Hebrew or Egyptian cultures.

Abel
Hebrew for 'breath' or 'son', Abel was the brother of Cain and the second son of Adam and Eve. The name is more common in France and Spain than in Britain.

Abraham: *Abe, Abie, Abram, Bram, Ham*
Abraham was another prominent Bible figure, but throughout history the name has never been very popular, except for a while in the Netherlands after the Reformation. Today it is more commonly used in America. In Hebrew it means 'father of nations'.

Ackerley
This very attractive, but seldom used, name meant 'from the fields where oak trees grow' in Old English.

Adam
God formed Adam out of red earth, and this is the meaning of the name. Adam was the first man, and his name has appeared throughout the ages. It has also been used as a basis for several surnames, examples being Adamson and MacAdam. In recent years it has become particularly popular.

Adrian
Coming from Latin, Adrian denotes 'the man from the Adriatic'. This was the name of the Roman Emperor, Hadrianus, who was responsible for building Hadrian's Wall across Northern England. Several popes have used Adrian as their official name, including the only English pope, Nicolas Breakspear of St Albans, who became Adrian IV in the twelfth century.

Aidan: *Aedan*
Meaning 'fire', Aidan is of Celtic origin.

Ainsley: *Ainslie, Ainsworth*
A quaint name originating from Mother Nature, Ainsley means 'from the meadow close by' in Old English.

Alastair: *Alasdair, Allister*
These are well-known Scottish derivatives of Alexander

Albert: *Adalbert, Adelbert, Al, Bert, Bertie*
Originaly Adalbert, meaning 'noble bright', this Old English name virtually disappeared to re-emerge as Albert. It remained rare except in Northern England and Scotland in the form Halbert, until Queen Victoria's marriage to Prince Albert of Saxe-Coburg-Gotha in the nineteenth century. Then it increased in popularity, particularly

amongst the poorer classes, as did the girl's name Alberta. Bert is the most common abbreviation of the name.

Aldous: *Aldis, Aldus*
The German name Aldo, meaning 'old', became popular in Italy and was Latinised as Aldus. There were three saints called Aldo: one Italian, one Scottish and one Belgian. In this country, Aldous is connected mainly with East Anglia, where the surnames derived from it, Aldhouse and Aldis, are most likely to be found.

Aldwin
From the Old English for 'old friend', this name gave rise to surnames such as Alden.

Alec: *Alex, Alick*
These were originally abbreviations of Alexander but are now given as independent names.

Alexander: *Alasdair, Alastair, Alec, Alex, Alick, Allister, Sacha, Sandy, Saunders*
Greek for 'protector' or 'defender of men', this name was given to Paris of Troy as an honour. It was tremendously popular in Europe in the Middle Ages, after the introduction of the Romance of Alisaundre, and also among the Indian Moslems, who were said to name many of their sons after Alexander the Great. There have been eight Pope Alexanders, and the name has also proved to be a favourite among royal families. It is particularly common in Scotland, where it was introduced in the eleventh century by Queen Margaret and became slightly altered to become Alasdair, Alistair, Allister and Sandy. From this come the surnames Saunders and Saunderson. Sacha, the Russian diminutive, is now used from time to time.

Alexis
Meaning 'defender', 'helper' or 'protector' in Greek, this was the name of a fifth-century saint. It is not very common as a Western name, although its popularity in Russia has in recent years led to its wider use in Britain, both as a girl's and a boy's name.

Alfred: *Alf, Alfie, Fred, Freddie*
From the Old English for 'elf counsel', it was Alfred the Great, who excelled as a statesman, a soldier and a scholar, who was the most famous bearer of this name. The Latinised version Alured continued in a minor way until as late as the eighteenth century, when Alfred, which had long since dropped from favour, was revived. Today it is gaining in popularity both in its full form and its diminutives.

Algernon: *Algie, Algy*
In the eleventh century the Counts of Boulogne, father and son, were distinguished by the fact that the son had a moustache and was known as Eustace 'aux gernons', which meant 'with the whiskers' in Norman French. Algernon has been used as a Christian name since the fifteenth century but has tended to remain in the upper classes, and today is not in common use.

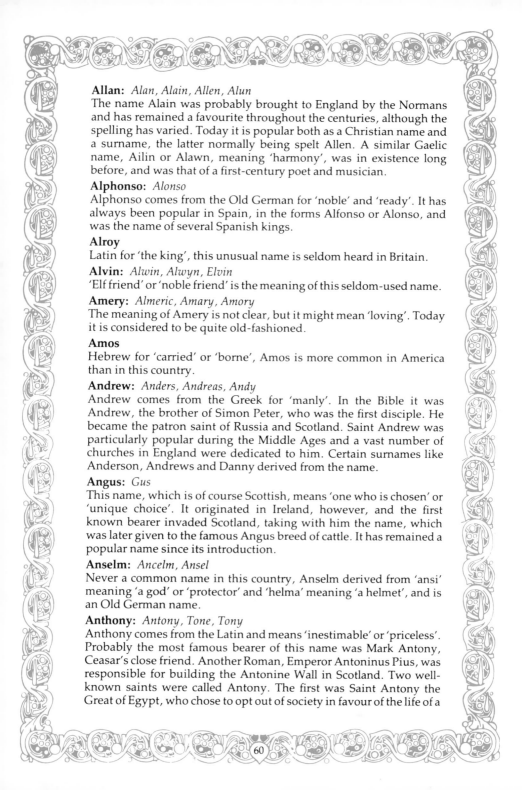

Allan: *Alan, Alain, Allen, Alun*

The name Alain was probably brought to England by the Normans and has remained a favourite throughout the centuries, although the spelling has varied. Today it is popular both as a Christian name and a surname, the latter normally being spelt Allen. A similar Gaelic name, Ailin or Alawn, meaning 'harmony', was in existence long before, and was that of a first-century poet and musician.

Alphonso: *Alonso*

Alphonso comes from the Old German for 'noble' and 'ready'. It has always been popular in Spain, in the forms Alfonso or Alonso, and was the name of several Spanish kings.

Alroy

Latin for 'the king', this unusual name is seldom heard in Britain.

Alvin: *Alwin, Alwyn, Elvin*

'Elf friend' or 'noble friend' is the meaning of this seldom-used name.

Amery: *Almeric, Amary, Amory*

The meaning of Amery is not clear, but it might mean 'loving'. Today it is considered to be quite old-fashioned.

Amos

Hebrew for 'carried' or 'borne', Amos is more common in America than in this country.

Andrew: *Anders, Andreas, Andy*

Andrew comes from the Greek for 'manly'. In the Bible it was Andrew, the brother of Simon Peter, who was the first disciple. He became the patron saint of Russia and Scotland. Saint Andrew was particularly popular during the Middle Ages and a vast number of churches in England were dedicated to him. Certain surnames like Anderson, Andrews and Danny derived from the name.

Angus: *Gus*

This name, which is of course Scottish, means 'one who is chosen' or 'unique choice'. It originated in Ireland, however, and the first known bearer invaded Scotland, taking with him the name, which was later given to the famous Angus breed of cattle. It has remained a popular name since its introduction.

Anselm: *Ancelm, Ansel*

Never a common name in this country, Anselm derived from 'ansi' meaning 'a god' or 'protector' and 'helma' meaning 'a helmet', and is an Old German name.

Anthony: *Antony, Tone, Tony*

Anthony comes from the Latin and means 'inestimable' or 'priceless'. Probably the most famous bearer of this name was Mark Antony, Ceasar's close friend. Another Roman, Emperor Antoninus Pius, was responsible for building the Antonine Wall in Scotland. Two well-known saints were called Antony. The first was Saint Antony the Great of Egypt, who chose to opt out of society in favour of the life of a hermit. He became known as the patron of swineherds and this gave rise to the term 'tantony' or 'Saint Antony' pig, which is the smallest of the litter. The second saint, Saint Antony of Padua, was a follower of Saint Francis of Assisi. The spelling Anthony appeared in the late sixteenth century and is commonly used in this country, although the 'h' remains silent, unlike the pronunciation of the name in America.

Archibald: *Arch, Archie, Baldie*
Coming from the Old German for 'truly bold', this name came to England with the Normans. It seems to have been well known in East Anglia and was frequently given to members of the East Anglian royal family. It gradually diminished in popularity in England, but became common in Scotland and has remained a favourite there to this day.

Arnold: *Arn, Arnie, Arny*
Arnold was introduced to Britain by the Normans, and was used in various forms both as a Christian and a surname before losing popularity in the seventeenth century. Recently it has been revived, and today is relatively common. It has a definite meaning, which is 'strong as an eagle'.

Arthur: *Art, Arty*
Arthur means 'strong as a bear'. An Irish chieftain and a Scottish king were the earliest known bearers of this name. Despite the renown of King Arthur of the Round Table, the name lost its appeal. Queen Victoria named her third son Arthur after his godfather, the Duke of Wellington, and as a result the name again became popular.

Ashley: *Lee*
A pleasant and popular name meaning 'one who dwells in the meadows of the ash tree'.

Aubrey: *Auberon*
Alberic, the legendary King of the Dwarfs, brought this name into being, hence its meaning, 'ruler of the elves'. The diminutive Auberon was first used in the thirteenth century and Shakespeare called one of his characters this in *A Midsummer Night's Dream*. Today neither name is much used.

Austin: *Aus, Austen*
Coming from Augustinus, Austin means 'exhalted', 'majestic' or 'His Majesty's subject'. There were two saints called Augustine, the better know of whom became the first Archbishop of Canterbury. The shortened version, Austin, appeared in the twelfth century, and although not popular for several centuries, still occurs occasionally.

B

Baldwin
Primarily a surname, Baldwin comes from the Old German for 'bold friend'. It was a popular surname in Flanders and became common in Britain in the forms Bowden, Boden and Bodkin as well as Baldwin.

Barnaby: *Barnabas, Barney*
Hebrew for 'son of exhortation', Barnabas was one of the Apostles who was a close companion of Saint Paul; he was stoned to death. The English form of the name is Barnaby, and today both Barnaby and Barney are fashionable names.

Barret: *Barrett*
Old German for 'bear rule', Barrett is better known as a surname than a Christian name.

Barry
Meaning 'spear' in Irish, this name is becoming increasingly popular in this country.

Bartholomew: *Bart, Barth, Bartley, Bate, Tolly*
This name, which comes from the Hebrew for 'sons of Talmai' (abounding in furrows), was first found in England in the twelfth century. This coincided with the beginnings of Saint Bartholomew's Hospital in London, which was founded by a court jester called Rahere, who was cured of injuries incurred in a fall after seeing a vision of Saint Bartholomew. It is common as a surname in various forms like Bateson, Batcock, Bartlet and Batty.

Basil
Basil comes from the Greek for 'kingly'. It was used mainly in the East, until the Crusaders introduced it to the West. It did not become particularly well known in Britain until the nineteenth century.

Benedict: *Ben, Bennett, Dixon*
From the Latin for 'blessed', Benedict was a name frequently taken by popes, and Saint Benedict, born in 480, gave his name to the religious order of monks the Benedictine Order. A number of surnames originate from Benedict, the most common of which are Benson, Bennett and Benn. Today the shortened version Ben is a pleasant and popular name.

Benjamin: *Ben, Benjie, Benjy, Benny, Benson*
This name, which comes from Hebrew, means 'son of my sorrow' (Ben Oni), or 'son of the right hand'. In the Bible, Benjamin was the younger brother of Joseph and son of Jacob. The name was not common during the Middle Ages, except among Jews, but after the Reformation it increased in popularity. Big Ben got its name from the first Commissioner of Works, who was Sir Benjamin Hall. Derivations are Benny, which is a popular Jewish name, and Bannerjee,

which is Indian. Today Ben is a name given to children in its own right, as well as the full name Benjamin.

Bernard: *Barnard, Barnett, Barney, Bernie*
Bernard is a name which comes from the German for 'as strong as a bear'. The bear was formerly considered to be sacred, being a very large and strong animal. The Saint Bernard dog was called after Saint Bernard of Menton, who founded the Alpine hospice for travellers in the tenth century. The name went out of fashion until it was revived during Queen Victoria's reign. Today Barney and Bernie are well-known derivations.

Bertram: *Bartram, Bert, Bertie, Bertrand*
Meaning 'bright raven', this Teutonic name quickly became fashionable in France as Bertrand, and in this country Bertram was particularly popular in the second half of the nineteenth century.

Bevan: *Bevin*
Celtic meaning 'warrior's son'.

Beverley
Beverley is well known for both men and women in Britain and comes from the Anglo-Saxon for 'ambitious'.

Bevis: *Bobo*
'One of beautiful appearance' is the meaning of this Old English name.

Bill: *Billy*
These are both well-known diminutives of William.

Blair
The name Blair is a strong and definite Celtic name meaning 'a place'.

Blake
The origin of Blake is not clear. As a surname its use is widespread but as a Christian name it is only chosen occasionally.

Boris
The most famous bearer of this Russian name was Boris Godunov, son-in-law of Ivan the Terrible, who became Tsar of Russia in the late 1500s. It means 'a warrior' or 'fighter'.

Boyce
Coming from the French, this means 'one who lives in the woods'.

Boyd
A popular name in recent years, Boyd means 'fair-haired'.

Bradley: *Brad*
Although more common as a surname, Bradley does exist as a first name and means 'one who comes from near the broad meadow'.

Brendan: *Brandon, Brennan*
A name with an unpleasant meaning, 'strongly smelling hair' or even 'stinking hair', and of Celtic origin. There is an early saint of the same name who founded the monastery of Clonfert in Ireland.

Brett
Meaning 'a Breton', native of Brittany, this name has, in recent years, become more popular.

Brian: *Brien, Bryan, Bryant*
Brian is thought to mean 'strong', although it is also connected with the word 'bre' meaning 'hill'. It seems to have been popular both in Ireland and Britain in early days, but gradually faded out in Britain until it was almost exclusively used in Ireland. Now it has re-emerged in this country and is commonly spelt Brian or Bryan.

Bruce
Thought to mean 'from the brushwood thicket', this name originated in a small village called Brieuse in Normandy, and was brought to this country by a companion of William the Conqueror. It has thrived mostly in Scotland.

Bruno
From the Old German 'brun', meaning 'brown', Bruno is rarely used as a first name in this country, although it is clear that the common surname Brown came from the same roots.

C

Callum
This is a surname that is occasionally used in Scotland as a Christian name and has become quite popular over the past few years.

Calvin: *Cal, Calvert*
Calvin comes from the Latin for 'having no hair'.

Cameron: *Cam*
Meaning 'crooked nose' in Gaelic, this name is fairly popular in Scotland as a Christian name, and very common as a surname.

Campbell
Derived from the French for 'from a bright field'.

Carl
This is a German derivative of Charles that is now popular as an independent name.

Carol
Unusual as a boy's name now, Carol, like Carl, evolved from Charles.

Carter: *Cart*
Carter is more common as a surname. It is Old English, meaning 'maker of carts'.

Casey
'Courageous' in Irish is the basis of this name.

Cecil: *Cec, Cis*
Latin for 'blind', this name was common in medieval England as a

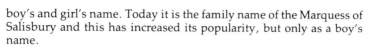

boy's and girl's name. Today it is the family name of the Marquess of Salisbury and this has increased its popularity, but only as a boy's name.

Cedric
Meaning 'friendly' in Celtic, this is thought to be an adaptation of Cerdic, who was an ancestor of the royal family.

Chad
'Battle' or 'war' is the meaning of this Anglo-Saxon name.

Chadwick
This name from the Celtic for 'guard' or 'defender' is probably more common today as a surname.

Charles: *Carl, Carol, Cary, Charley, Charlie, Chas, Chuck, Karl*
From the Old German for 'a man', this name first became very popular in Europe owing to the fame of either Charles the Great or Charlemagne. The Normans brought it to England, and since the time when it was used by members of the Stuart family it has increased in popularity, particularly in Scotland. It is also a surname.

Chester: *Cheston, Chet*
Chester comes from the Latin for 'of the stronghold'.

Christian: *Chris, Christy, Kit, Kristian, Kristin*
Latin for 'a Christian', this was the name of ten Danish kings. Until recently it has not been common in this country but it is now quite fashionable.

Christopher: *Chippy, Chris, Christie, Christy, Kester, Kit, Kris*
Christopher means 'the bearer of Christ' in Greek. Christians formerly used the word to mean that they held Christ within their hearts. Saint Christopher, according to legend, carried Christ as a child across a stream, and since then he has become associated with travel. In Catholic countries the image of the saint is commonly carried by people going on journeys, as it is supposed to protect them from accidents or untimely death.

Clarence: *Clare, Clarry*
The meaning of the name Clarence is obscure; however, it possibly originated from the Latin 'clarus', meaning 'famous', 'bright' or 'clear'. The title Duke of Clarence has been used in the royal family, but Clarence was not used as a Christian name until towards the end of the nineteenth century.

Clark
Latin for 'knowledgeable', Clark is not a name that has caught on in Britain.

Claud: *Claude. Claudie*
Meaning 'limping' in Latin, Claude has always been popular in France, and to a lesser extent in Spain and Italy. It is more common in Scotland than in England.

Clement: *Clem, Clemence*
One of the disciples of Saint Paul was Saint Clement, and several popes took this name also. It means 'merciful' or 'mild', and for many generations has been a popular name, both in its full form and in the shortened version Clem. Surnames such as Clemson and Clements came from this name.

Clifford: *Cliff*
Several villages of this name in England, which are situated on slopes or hills near rivers with fords, have given rise to Clifford, which in its full form is more common as a surname. However, the diminutive, Cliff, is fast coming into its own as a popular first name for boys.

Clive
'Cliff' is the meaning of this name, which became popular because of General Robert Clive of India. British families living in India are first thought to have used it as a Christian name.

Colin: *Cole*
Coming from France, Colin was a diminutive of Nicholas. However, it is also believed to have connections with the Celtic word 'cailean', meaning 'young dog'. Possibly the collie dog may have got its name from the same root. It is a popular surname in the form Collin(s) or Collinson.

Conan: *Conran*
Celtic, meaning 'high', 'intelligent', this name is today more popular in Ireland than in Britain. Probably the most well-known person of this name was Sir Arthur Conan Doyle, who created 'Sherlock Holmes'.

Connor: *Conor*
This name is more favoured in Ireland, featuring greatly in Irish mythology and meaning 'high desire'.

Conrad: *Con, Connie, Curt, Konrad*
This comes from the Old German 'conja rad' and means 'strong counsel'. It was the name of the tenth-century saint and is more commonly used in Germany than in Britain.

Craig
This short name, which is popular today, comes from the Celtic and means ' from the stony hill, or crag'.

Crispin: *Crispen, Crispian*
Coming from the Latin and meaning 'curly-haired', Crispin is a seldom-used name.

Curtis
Another name that is more used as a surname, Curtis comes from the French, meaning 'courteous'.

Cuthbert: *Cuthburt*
Cuthbert means 'celebrated' and was the name of a seventh-century

saint. During the 1914-18 war it was used as a slang term for a person who avoided doing his military service. Today it is not common.

Cyril
Greek for 'lordly' or 'masterful', there were several saints who took this name; however, it did not become used in this country until the nineteenth century.

D

Dale: *Dalton*
Dale denotes a person who lives in the valley in Old German. This is a well-known name today.

Damian
Thought to come from the Greek Damianos, meaning to 'subdue' or 'domesticate', Damian has been used as a Christian name in this country since the eleventh century.

Damon: *Damian, Damien*
Greek, from the same root as Damian, this means 'the tamer'.

Daniel: *Dan, Danny Daniell, Darnell*
Daniel was one of the great prophets, and in the Bible we read the famous story of him being cast into the lion's den because of his faith and emerging completely unharmed. It was a very popular name in the thirteenth and fourteenth centuries and today is increasing in popularity once again. It comes from the Hebrew for 'God has judged'.

Darren: *Darrol, Darryl*
Darren is an Old English name meaning 'dearly loved'.

David: *Dave, Davis, Davy*
Hebrew for 'beloved' or 'darling'. In the Bible we read how David slayed the giant Goliath. He later became King of Israel. There was a saint called David who became the patron saint of Wales and there have been two Scottish kings with this name. The surnames David, Davidson, Dawes and Dawkins are derived from David. The Welsh version of the name is Dewi.

Dean
Dean is an Old English name meaning 'dale' or 'vale'.

Denis: *Dennis, Dennison, Denny, Denys, Denzil*
Denis comes from the Greek 'Dionysius', which means 'the divine one from Nysa'. Dionysos, or Bacchus, was the god of wine. Several saints had this name, including the patron saint of France, Saint Denys. From this name we get the surnames Tennyson, Dennison and Dennis. Introduced into England in the twelfth century, the name went out of fashion for a while, but since the beginning of the twentieth century has been fairly common.

Denzil: *Danzil*
This is the name of a place in Cornwall and has always had Cornish connections. The meaning is uncertain but is thought to be connected with the Cornish word 'uhel', which means 'high'.

Derek: *Derk, Derrick, Dirk, Rick*
A derivative of the German name Theodoric, this means 'ruler of the people'. Popular in the fifteenth century, the name went rapidly out of favour in the seventeenth century, and some say this was because of a well-known hangman of that time. Today the name is popular in several different spellings — Deryk, Deric, and Dirk, which is a variation of the Dutch form.

Dermot: *Diarmuit, Diarmid*
Dermot cames from Ireland and means 'free from envy'. Legend tells us that Diarmaid was the lover of Grainne, Queen of Tara. Her husband forced him to hunt a wild boar and he was killed. A shortened version of the name is Derby, hence the phrase 'Derby and Joan', which describes a happy elderly couple.

Derwin: *Derr, Dorwin, Durwin, Win*
Coming from the Old German for 'a lover of animals', this is not a common name at present.

Desmond: *Desi*
Irish, meaning 'a man from South Munster'. This was a surname long before it became used as a Christian name, which first occurred in Ireland, and more recently in this country.

Dexter
In Latin Dexter means 'skilful' or 'right-handed'.

Digby
A name that is gaining in popularity at present, Digby is Old English for 'from the people living by the dyke'.

Dinsdale
Dinsdale means 'he who was born on the Sabbath' in Welsh.

Dominic: *Dom, Dominey, Dominick, Nick, Nicky*
'The day of the Lord' or 'a child born on Sunday' are the meanings of this name, which comes from the Latin 'dies dominica'. Saint Dominic was the founder of the order of friars known as the Dominicans, or Black Friars (so called because of the black cloaks they wore). Hence the area in London where their monastery stood is known as the district of Blackfriars. After the Reformation the name died out except among Catholics, but it is now gaining in popularity once again.

Donald: *Don, Donal, Donnie, Donny*
A Gaelic name meaning 'mighty in the world' or 'ruler of the world', Donald was the name of no less than six Scottish kings. It is an extremely popular name in Scotland, as is the Irish equivalent, Donal. There is an old Celtic name Donn that means 'brown'; however, the

diminutive Don, which is much used today, is the shortened form of Donald.

Dougal

This is a commonly used name in Scotland today, although it originates in Ireland, and means 'dark stranger'. Apparently the Irish used to call Norwegians by this name.

Douglas: *Doug, Duggie*

At one time Douglas was a place-name; the best translation of the meaning is 'dark water'. Certainly, Douglas in the Isle of Man took its name from its dark water. The name was not common before the sixteenth century; however, towards the end of that century it had become equally popular both for girls and boys. Now only given to boys, it is popular once more. It is also found as a surname.

Dudley: *Dud, Lee*

Dudley is simply the name of a place in Worcestershire, and was an artistocratic surname from the time of the Tudor dynasty. Now it is also used as a first name, although it is still only creeping into general use and is not at present very popular.

Duncan: *Dunc*

There were two famous Scottish kings called Duncan, one of whom is better known than the other because of Shakespeare's drama *Macbeth*. It is an Old Irish name that means 'brown soldier'.

Dunstan

An unusual name with an unusual meaning—'hill rock'. One of the Archbishops of Canterbury during the Middle Ages was called Dunstan.

Dwight

In Britain, Dwight is used only as a surname; in America, however, it is fairly common as a Christian name. The meaning and origins are uncertain but it is thought that it might mean 'fair' or 'light'.

Dylan

A Welsh name, and probably the best-known bearer of the name is Dylan Thomas, the famous poet. It is also the name of a legendary Welsh hero.

E

Eamon

See Edmund, since Eamon is the Irish form of this name.

Earl: *Earle, Erle, Errol*

This name has become popular in more recent years, in particular in America. It comes from the Old English and means 'nobleman'.

Edgar: *Ed, Eddie, Eddy*

Old English for 'prosperous spear', Edgar was in early times a regal name, and was the name of the first king of England to be publicly acknowledged. Up until the end of the thirteenth century Edgar was fairly popular. Then it faded out until last century. Today it is not very common among the younger generation.

Edmond: *Eamon, Ed, Eddie, Edmund, Ned*
Two famous kings and two saints share this grand name, which means 'richly guarded' or 'happily protected'. Edmund existed largely as a name belonging to the royal family and certain better-known families, and in this way it has survived the generations. The Irish version, Eamon, is fairly common.

Edric: *Dric, Edrick*
This unusual name is Old English and means 'prosperous ruler'. Today it is not in common use.

Edson: *Edison*
Naturally enough, Edson means 'son of Ed'. It is probably better known in the form Edison and is more common as a surname.

Edward: *Ed, Eddie, Ned, Neddie, Ted, Teddy*
Edward and Edmond have the same meaning. However, Edward has always been more popular than Edmond. Several kings were called Edward, the most famous being Edward the Confessor, who was the last Saxon king. It is a name that has spanned all classes of society throughout the ages and has never gone out of fashion. It is also of interest that Edward is one of the few names of English origin that has spread to other countries.

Edwin: *Ed, Eddie, Eddy, Edwyn*
'Rich' or 'happy' 'friend', Saint Edwin was the first Christian king of Northumbria, who is said to have given his name to Edinburgh (Edwin's Burgh). Although it was initially a common name, by the twelfth century it had become rare except as a surname. It was revived during the reign of Queen Victoria. Today it is not in common use.

Eldon: *El, Elden*
The meaning of this Anglo-Saxon name is obscure, but is thought to be either 'the vale of elves' or 'one who is highly esteemed'.

Eli: *Ely*
A short name, popular among those of Jewish faith, Eli means 'the highest'. From the Bible we learn that Eli was the high priest who educated the prophet Samuel. It became used among Christians as a first name in the seventeenth century.

Elias: *Elijah, El(l)iot(t), Ellis*
Another Hebrew name, meaning 'Jehovah is God'. It is probably more common in the form Elijah, which again is a name from the Bible. Eliot and Ellis, other derivations, have been common in this country for many years, in particular as surnames, although Eliot is coming into more frequent use. The French equivalent, Élie, is still popular across the Channel.

Elmer

Although this is a common name in America, it does have Anglo-Saxon roots and means 'noble fame'. It can also be spelt Almer. It has been used as a surname, and today it is not a popular first name in this country.

Elton

This comes from the Old English and meaning 'one who dwells at the old farm or village'.

Elvin: *Elwin*

Perhaps more commonly spelt Alvin, this name means 'elf friend'. It is a quaint, but not common name.

Elvis

'One who is all-wise' is the meaning of this name, which has been made popular by the famous rock artist, Elvis Presley.

Emanuel: *Emmanuel, Immanuel, Manny*

In the Bible we read that this is the name given to Jesus, the Son of God, and it is therefore not surprising that it is a Hebrew name meaning 'God is with us'. The Greeks were the first nation to use it as a Christian name, and it quickly spread to other European countries. It is particularly popular in Spain and Portugal in the forms Manuel or Manoel. In this country it has never been a common name, except among Jews, and they are known to use the attractive abbreviation Manny.

Emery: *Emerick, Emory*

Emery comes from the Old German, and is thought to mean 'ruler'. Until the late eighteenth century it was used infrequently both for boys and girls. Today the female version is Emerica, and the male version Emery or Emerick is still uncommon.

Emile: *Emil*

'One who strives or works hard', Emile is not a popular name at present.

Emlyn

A Welsh name; the origins are obscure. However, it might have come from the Latin name 'Aemilianus'.

Enoch

Apparently Enoch was one of Adam's descendants in the Bible, the father of Methuselah. For several centuries now it has been used as a Christian name but has never been greatly in vogue.

Eric: *Erick, Erik, Rickie*

'One who rules' is the most accepted meaning of Eric, which is a common Scandinavian name, and was brought to England by the Danes. Many Danish and Swedish kings had this name. In this country it is fairly common.

Ernest: *Ern, Ernie*

Earnest is the meaning of this name, although it also means 'vigour'.

It is German in origin, and has always been popular among the aristocracy there. It has only really been common in Britain for about 130 years as a first name.

Esmond
Old English for 'gracious protector', Esmond has always been rare, and today is not often chosen as a first name for a son.

Eugene: *Gene*
No less than four popes have taken the name Eugene, which means 'one who is born lucky'. It was also a royal name found in early Scottish history, and in Ireland it has replaced Eoin, which was the Irish version of John. It is more common in America than in Britain, where it is often abbreviated to Gene.

Eustace
From the Greek and meaning 'fruitful', there were two saints called Eustace. The better known was a patron saint of huntsmen, who is said to have been converted while hunting. He was generally fairly popular, hence his name became frequently used during the Middle Ages, in particular in France. The name was brought to England by the Normans, but has never been very popular in this country.

Evan
This is the Welsh of John.

Everard: *Ev, Everett*
'Strong as a boar' is the meaning of this German name, which is rare as a first name in Britain but more frequently heard as a surname in the form Everitt.

Ewen: *Ewan, Ewin*
This Scottish name used to be popular in England, but today is rarely heard outside Scotland.

Ezra: *Ez*
Hebrew for 'helper', this name is occasionally heard in England and America.

F

Fabian: *Fabe, Fabyan*
Latin in origin, it is thought that Fabian may mean 'bean grower'. It has never been very common, although there was a pope of this name.

Fairfax
Old English, meaning 'one with fair hair'.

Fairley: *Fairlie, Farley*
Another Old English name, meaning 'from the distant pasture'.

Felix

Felix, meaning 'happy' in Latin, was the name of several saints and four popes. One of the saints gave his name to Felixstowe, in East Anglia. Today, the girl's version, Felicity, is more common, although Felix is in use in this country.

Ferdinand: *Ferd, Ferdie, Fernand, Fernando*

This is a name that is more frequently used on the Continent, in particular in France, Spain and Italy. But it was the origin of surnames like Farrant and Farrand, which are more common in Britain than Ferdinand as a first name.

Fergus: *Fergie*

'One who has been chosen' is the meaning of this name, which is most popular in Scotland, and to a lesser extent in Ireland. It is not often heard in England. The surname Ferguson is more common in the northern parts of Britain.

Finlay

The majority of boys' names beginning with the letter F seem to be unusual and Finlay is no exception. It means 'fair hero' and is more often heard as a surname than a first name.

Flavian: *Flavius*

Latin for 'blond' or 'yellow-haired'.

Floyd: *Lloyd*

Celtic for 'grey' or 'dark', Floyd and Lloyd are not common first names in this country.

Foster

More common as a surname, Foster means 'forester' and is German in origin.

Francis: *Frank, Frankie, Franz*

Saint Francis of Assisi, who is famous for his great love of animals and also for forming the group of friars who became known as the Franciscans, must have made his name popular throughout the ages. It means 'the Frenchman', and Frank is common as a shortened version.

Frank: *Frankie*

Frank is believed to exist in its own right as a full name, and in fact probably originated before Francis. It means 'the free man'. In Britain it was scarcely heard of in olden days except as a diminutive of Francis.

Franklin: *Frank*

Obviously coming from the same root as Frank, Franklin also means 'a free man' or 'a freeholder'. It is both a surname and a first name.

Fraser: *Frasier. Frazer*

Fraser is thought to come either from the Old English, meaning 'curly-haired', of from the Old French, meaning 'strawberry'. It is popular in Scotland.

Frederick: *Fred, Freddie, Frederic, Fritz*
'Peaceful ruler' is the meaning of this name, which originates from the Old German. It was very popular in Germany, but until the seventeenth century hardly existed in any form in Britain. Once here, it grew in popularity until in the nineteenth century it was one of the most common names for boys. The shortened versions Fred and Freddie are today popular.

Fulton
Old English for 'coming from a farm or field', Fulton is more generally a surname, except in Scotland where it is a Christian name.

G

Gabriel: *Gabby, Gabe, Gabryell*
Hebrew for 'strong man of God', it was the angel Gabriel who announced to the Virgin Mary that she was to give birth to Jesus. It has never been a very popular name in Britain.

Galvin: *Vin*
A name which means 'a sparrow'. It is not in common use as a first name.

Gareth: *Garth*
'A gardener' or 'from the garden' are thought to be the meanings of these two names, although the origins are rather obscure. Gareth is used frequently in Wales. Garth, which is thought to be a derivation of Gareth, is used today as a name in its own right.

Garret: *Garrard, Garrett, Garry, Gary, Gerard*
A name not heard often nowadays, Garret means 'one who is firm with a spear'. It has the same meaning and derivations as Gerard, which is a more common boy's name.

Gaston
A name with a French flavour to it, Gaston means 'the man from Gascony'. It is very popular in France and occasionally heard in Britain.

Gavin: *Gavan, Gawain, Gawen*
'From the field of the hawk', Gawain was the nephew of King Arthur according to the tales of the Round Table. This Welsh version of the name has not survived so well as the Scottish Gavin.

Geoffrey: *Geoff, Jeff, Jeffrey, Jeffry*
Although Jeffrey is the older version of this name, the more common spelling today is Geoffrey. There are three possible origins of the name, so there are several variations in meaning, the most popular of which seems to be 'God's peace'. It might also mean 'traveller in a land that is peaceful'. Godfrey is another version of the same name.

George: *Geordie, Georgie, Georgy*

Saint George was a Roman soldier who was put to death because he was a Christian. Although little is known about him, he became the patron saint of England, and a legend of him fighting with a dragon has made him famous despite the lack of historical evidence. In early times, George was not at all popular. Until the four Hanoverian King Georges (one of whom was Georgie Porgie), since then the name has always been popular in Britain. There have been six kings called George. In Scotland and northern England the pet name for George is Georgie, and from this we get the colloquial term by which the inhabitants of Tyneside are known Geordies. George means 'tiller of the land' or 'farmer'.

Gerald: *Gerold, Gerry, Jerry*

Old German for 'mighty spear' or 'spear force'. It was a popular name in all parts of Britain until the thirteenth century, when it died out in England. However, it was revived towards the end of the last century, probably being reintroduced from Ireland, and today is fairly popular again. It is sometimes confused with the name Gerard.

Gerard: *Gerry, Jerrard, Jerry*

Coming from the same origins as Gerald, Gerard means 'spear hard'. In the Middle Ages it was a common name, and from it several surnames have originated; for example, Garret, Garrett and Garrard. Today it is not as popular a name as Gerald.

Gerbert

Another name from the same root as the previous two names. This one means 'bright spear'. It is not in frequent use in this country.

German

There were two saints of this name, which means 'a German'. It has not been in common use in this country for many years, although occasionally one comes across surnames that have originated from it; for example, Germain, Jermyn.

Gervais: *Gervase, Jarvis, Jervis*

'Servant of the spear' is the meaning of this unusual name. The surnames that come from it, Jarvis and Jarvie, are better known.

Gideon

This name has rather a sad meaning: 'one handed' or 'having a stump'. It is Hebrew in origin and is more common in America than in Britain.

Giffard: *Gifford*

'Fierce gift' is the meaning of this little-used name, which was popular in past generations.

Gilbert: *Bert, Gib, Gil, Gilpin*

Another name giving rise to different surnames, Gilbert comes from the Old German and means 'bright pledge'. The most common surnames originating from it are Gilbertson, Gibbs, Gibson, Gilby. One of the saints of this name, Saint Gilbert of Sempringham, founded the religious order known as the Gilbertines. In Scotland it has always been a popular name.

Giles: *Gil*
Saint Giles was a Greek from Athens who went to France to become a hermit. He is the patron saint of beggars and cripples, and also of Edinburgh. It is interesting that some of the poorest areas in towns are named after him; for example, St Giles in London was originally a very poor quarter, as was St Giles' in Oxford. There are well over 100 churches dedicated to this saint in England. Giles means 'kid'; that is, baby goat.

Gilmour
From the Old English, this name means 'servant of St Mary'.

Gilroy
'Servant of the king' is the meaning of this name, which today is not in common use.

Glen: *Glenn, Glyn, Glynn*
Welsh for 'valley', this name is gaining in popularity in this country.

Godfrey
Godfrey means 'God's peace' and in the Middle Ages was a common name. It later became confused with Geoffrey and today it is Geoffrey which is the more popular name.

Godwin: *Goodwin*
Meaning 'dear' or 'faithful' 'friend', Godwin was in former days one of the best-known Christian names. Today it is a more common surname in one of the following forms: Goodwin, Godden, Godding and Goding.

Gordon
This is the name of a place in Berwickshire, home of a famous Scottish family. Until the time of General Gordon of Khartoum it was not used as a first name. Today it is a pleasant and popular name, used frequently both in Scotland and England.

Graham: *Graeme*
This, like the previous name, is that of a famous Scottish family and place-name, although it is said to mean 'from the grey house'. It is in common use.

Grant
'The great one' or 'the tall one' is the meaning of this name, which comes from the French. It was originally used only as a surname, but lately it has become popular as a first name.

Granville: *Grenville*
Another French name, meaning 'from the large town', it came from Granville in Normandy. It is also used as a surname.

Gregory: *Greg*
Sixteen popes took this name, beginning with Saint Gregory the Great in the sixth century. It means 'vigilant' of 'watchful', and up

until the Reformation was a popular name. It has given rise to a number of surnames; for example, Gregson, Griggs, Greig, Gregory, and of course the Scottish McGregor.

Griffith: *Griffin, Rufus*
This name means either 'chief' ('lord') or 'red-haired'. It is most popular in Wales and apparently there were several Welsh princes called Griffith. It is also used as a surname.

Gustav: *Gus, Gussie, Gustavus*
The meaning of this name is somewhat obscure but is thought to be of Scandinavian origin, meaning 'to meditate'. It is a name more often connected with the Continent — Gustaf in Sweden, Gustav in Germany and Gustave in France. It has rarely been used in this country but may well grow in popularity in the years to come.

Guy
Guy is thought to be Old German in origin, meaning either 'wood' or 'wide'. It was a well-known name in this country until the infamous Guy Fawkes caused it to drop rapidly from fashion. It is now coming back into common use.

H

Hadwin: *Hadwyn, Wynn*
This unusual name means 'battle friend'.

Hamilton
Better known as a surname, Hamilton has several different meanings, the most accepted of which is 'the home-lover's property'.

Hamish
This is the Gaelic form of James. It is most common in Scotland.

Hamon: *Hamelen, Hamo*
Old German for 'house' or 'home', Hamon was formerly a very popular name, being brought to England by the Normans. Hamlet appears to be a derivative of the name. It has lost popularity and today is practically never heard.

Hansel
Scandinavian in origin, Hansel, though little used, is well known today because of the famous fairy tale about two children, Hansel and Gretel.

Harley: *Arley, Harden, Hart, Hartley*
This quaint Old English name is not often heard as a first name. It means 'coming from the meadow of hares'.

Harold: *Hal, Harald, Harrold, Harry, Herald, Herrick*
'Ruler of the army' is the meaning of this Old English name. It also has

Scandinavian connections, since there have been several King Harolds in Norway, Denmark and Sweden. After being a popular name, it almost died out until the nineteenth century, when it was revived. It is not very common today.

Hartley
A surname that came from a place-name and has now become a Christian name, Hartley means 'stag meadow'.

Harvey: *Harv, Harve, Herv*
Harvey is thought to mean either 'bitter' of 'fighter in an army'. It comes from the Breton 'Haerveu', and there was a fifth-century Breton saint of this name. He was blind and a poet. Today it is not often heard as a first name, although the surname Harvey is fairly widespread.

Hedley
Originally a surname, Hedley has in recent years been introduced as a Christian name, especially in Cornwall.

Henry: *Hal, Hank, Harry, Hendrick, Henri*
For many years Harry or Herry was the most popular version of this name, although it was mostly the aristocrats who used it. Today Harry is merely a diminutive of Henry and not a name in its own right. As well as the eight English King Henrys, there were several French kings of this name and some German emperors. The present pet names from Henry are Hal or Harry, and to a lesser extent Hank, which has come over from America. The meaning of Henry is 'the ruler of the home, or estate'.

Herbert: *Bert, Bertie, Herb, Herbie*
'Bright warrior' is the meaning of this name, which until the nineteenth century was never popular in this country. Until recently it was a most fashionable name, but its popularity has diminished over the past two decades and today is not frequently used.

Hereward
Hereward the Wake, the last Saxon leader to attack the Normans, is the most famous bearer of this unusual name. It is thought to mean 'protector of the army'.

Herman: *Armin, Armond, Herm, Hermie, Hermon*
Coming from the same origin as Herbert, Herman is Old German for 'army man' or 'warrior'. One of its derivatives, which came by way of France, is Armin, and this, although as rare as Herman itself, was found recently in Norfolk.

Hilary: *Hillary, Hillery*
Hilary is both a girl's name and a boy's name and comes from the Latin for 'cheerful' — hence our own word 'hilarious'. Suprisingly, it was as a man's name that it has survived through the generations, the feminine version almost dying out at the beginning of this century. Now, however, Hilary is more popular for girls than boys.

Hiram: *Hy*

'God is high' is the meaning of this Hebrew name. Unusual and interesting, it is more popular in America than in this country.

Horace: *Horatio, Horry*

The famous Latin poet Horace is the reason for this name surviving. It seems to be something of a family name, passed down the generations in only a few well-to-do families. Nobody is clear as to its meaning, but possibly it is connected with time, since 'hora' in Latin means 'hour'.

Howard: *Howie*

This is yet another name that began its life as a surname, and has only relatively recently come into use as a first name. Today it is popular and thriving, and has lost any aristocratic connections that it once had. Its meaning is a little dubious, but thought to be either 'protection' in some form or other, or 'heart'.

Howell: *Hywel*

Hywel is the Welsh version of the more fashionable Howell. 'Distinguished' is its meaning, and gives the name a feeling of strength and majesty.

Hubert: *Hubie, Hugh*

Saint Hubert was a huntsman who became a popular patron saint in the eighth century. His saint's day is 3 November, which was the day on which stag-hunting would begin, during the days when virtually the only fresh meat available in winter was venison. Another form of the same name was Hubard, hence our nursery rhyme 'Old Mother Hubbard'. 'Shining heart or mind' is said to be the meaning of Hubert.

Hugh: *Hew, Huey, Hughie, Hugo*

'Heart', 'spirit' or 'inspiration' are all meanings of Hugh or Hugo, which have given rise to a large number of surnames, the most popular of which are Hughes, Hew, Hewlitt and Howe. Today both Hugh and Hugo are common in most parts of Britain.

Humphrey: *Humfrey, Humfry*

From the Old German for 'peace' or 'protector of peace'.

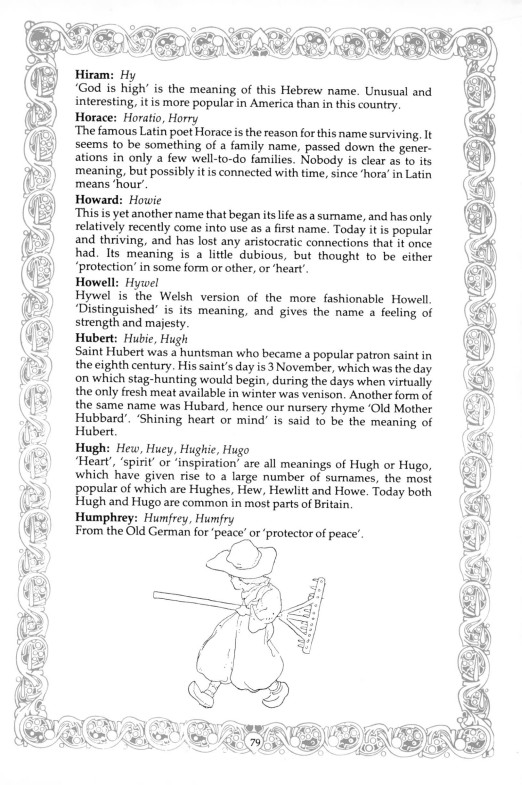

I

Ian: *Iain*
Ian is the Scottish equivalent of John. Iain is the more Gaelic version.

Ignatius
The fame of the sixteenth-century Spanish Saint Ignatius Loyola led to the spread of this name in Europe. In England it is used mainly by Roman Catholic families. Its meaning is 'fiery'.

Ike
This is a pet name for Isaac; at present quite a well-known diminutive.

Ilbert
Originally from the Old German for 'strife' and 'bright', it was the Normans who brought this name to Britain.

Ingram
Another name introduced by the Normans, Ingram comes from the German for 'angel's raven'. Nowadays it is often associated with its use as a surname.

Inigo
This name appears in the Bible as that of the Bishop of Antioch, who was the author of letters to churches in Asia Minor. In the West its use was confined to Spain, where it is still popular in its derivative form Ignatius. Inigo Jones, the seventeenth-century English architect and theatrical designer is the most well known holder of this name.

Irving
Although originally a surname, this has recently been given as a Christian name as in the case of the modern American composer Irving Berlin. The meaning of the name is given as 'friend of the sea'.

Isaac: *Ike*
Hebrew for 'laughter', this name is well known for its biblical connections but less for its modern usage. Although in use in this country since before the Norman Conquest it has enjoyed only one brief period of popularity, which was in the sixteenth century after the Reformation.

Ivan
A Russian form of John that is now quite well known.

Ivor: *Ifor*
Ivor is a Celtic name popular in Ireland and Scotland, and also in Wales, where it is spelt Ifor. It may have come originally from the Scandinavian name Ivarr.

J

Jack
This is a very well established pet form of John that is sometimes used as a name in its own right, particularly in America. It is the basis of the surname Jackson.

Jacob
Jacob was the name of Isaac's younger son in the Bible story and comes from the Hebrew for 'a supplanter'. Although there were two apostles of this name it was rarely used in this country until after the Reformation, when it appeared in English translations of the Bible. It is, however, the root from which James eventually developed.

Jake
A pet name for James used since the early fourteenth century, and not unknown as a given name.

James: *Hamish, Jake, Jamie, Jim, Jimmy, Seamus, Sean, Shane*
In Britain James was the popular development from Jacob. It began to be used in the early thirteenth century after the first pilgrimages to the shrine of Saint James 'the Greater' at Compostella in Spain. Saint James was one of the twelve apostles and brother of Saint John, who was martyred in A.D.44. Although used in surnames such as James, Jameson and Fitzjames, use as a Christian name was not widespread until after James Stuart became King of England in 1603, and it has been a favourite since then.

Jason
The name of the writer of the Book of Ecclesiasticus was translated into English as Jason. Although it has been used quite frequently in America since the seventeenth century it has only recently become popular in Britain. It is thought to mean 'the healer'.

Jasper
Persian for 'master of the treasure'. Jasper is the English version of Gaspar, one of the legendary wise men to visit Jesus at his birth. It has been used occasionally since the fourteenth century, sometimes as a surname.

Jeffrey: *Geoffrey, Jeffery*
Originally from the German for 'traveller in a peaceful land', these are alternative spellings of the name Geoffrey.

Jeremy: *Jeremiah, Jerry*
From the Hebrew for 'God has appointed', the name Jeremy developed from Jeremiah, that of one of the great prophets. The name Jeremiah itself was revived by the Puritans and is still popular in Southern Ireland, where the prophet himself was supposed to have visited.

Jerome
This means 'holy name' in Greek. It was Saint Jerome's translation of the Bible into Latin that formed the basis of the Vulgate.

Jesse
From the Hebrew for 'the Lord is', Jesse was first used as a Christian name in the sixteenth century.

Jethro
Another name used since the Reformation, Jethro comes from the Hebrew for 'abundance' or 'excellence'.

Jevon
This is an unusual Welsh version of John.

Joel
Hebrew for 'the Lord is God', this name, which has mainly been used in the last four centuries, was a Breton name introduced at the time of the Norman Conquest.

John: *Evan, Iain, Ian, Ivan, Jack, Jevon, Jon, Zane*
This favourite choice among boys' names means 'God is gracious'. Well known as the name of both the Apostle and the Evangelist in the Bible, and consequently of numerous churches throughout England, John has been particularly well used since the eighteenth century. A great many surnames developed from it, such as Johnson, Jones, Jackson, Jenkins and Jennings.

Jonah
An unusual name from the Hebrew for 'dove'.

Jonathan
Meaning 'God has given a son' in Hebrew, Jonathan has been used mainly since the Reformation.

Jordan
Probably from the German for 'land', use of this old name was established after crusaders brought back holy water from the river Jordan to baptise their children. At present it is more common in America.

Joseph: *Joe*
Meaning 'may the Lord increase the children', this biblical name has been particularly popular since the seventeenth century. It was originally used to name children after the favourite son of Jacob and Sarah, but most people now would associate Joseph with the father of Jesus.

Joshua
From the Hebrew for 'God is my salvation', Joshua is a variation in translation of the name Jesus, and it is the one that has been used in Britain. In Spanish-speaking countries Jesus is the better-known version.

Jude
This is a contraction of the biblical name Judas, and since it is not

immediately connected with the unfortunate Judas Iscariot it is more acceptable. It means 'God leads'.

Julian

This name has derived from Julius, meaning 'downy' in Greek. It has been used since the thirteenth century and several surnames have developed from it, such as Jolland and Golland. The most popular saint of this name was Saint Julian 'The Hospitaller', a patron saint of travellers.

Justin

From the Latin for 'just', Justin is becoming more popular now. It was Justinian I, a sixth-century Byzantine emperor, a successful campaigner in North Africa and Italy, who wrote a legal code which later became the basis of Roman law.

K

Karl

This was the original German form of Charles, meaning 'a man', which has recently been reintroduced.

Kean

This is a Celtic name meaning 'vast'.

Keith

Although well known in England now, Keith was just a Scottish family name that derived from a place-name.

Kenelm

Local to the Midlands, Kenelm is a name that comes from the Celtic for 'valiant helmet'.

Kenneth: *Ken, Kenny*

From the Gaelic for 'a leader', this was mainly a Scottish name until taken up in England during the last hundred years. Kenneth was the name of the first king of Scotland, and it was his victory over the Picts that made him the traditional founder of the Kingdom of Scotland.

Kenrick

Anglo-Saxon for 'royal ruler', this was a well-known name in the Middle Ages.

Kester

Kester was originally a diminutive of Christopher, first used around the seventeenth century.

Kevin

Kevin is an Irish name meaning 'pleasant birth', particularly common in that country due to the influence of Saint Kevin. It is also used widely in Britain nowadays.

Kieron: *Kieren*
These names come from the Celtic for 'black' or 'dark'.
Kim
Kim comes from the Old English for 'ruler'.
Kirk
A modern name from the Scottish for a church, more common in America than in Britain.

L

Lambert
From an Old German name for 'bright land', Lambert was fairly common in the Middles Ages and has been used occasionally since then.

Lance: *Lancelot*
Meaning 'land' in German, Lance became more popular from the thirteenth century onwards in its diminutive form of Lancelot, a name well known for its connection with the King Arthur legends. Lance is the more usual version now.

Laurence: *Larry, Laurie, Lawrence*
This comes from the Latin for 'a bay tree'. Before the Norman invasion Laurence was a name used by monks, after that, however, it became very popular and several surnames developed from it. It has been a favourite name in Ireland since the twelfth century, when Saint Laurence O'Toole was Archbishop of Dublin. In the twentieth century the name gained considerable renown from the exploits of 'Lawrence of Arabia', although in this case it was a surname.

Lee: *Leigh*
From the Anglo-Saxon for 'a meadow', this became a common surname. In the nineteenth century it began to be used as a Christian name in America and it is now also used in Britain.

Leo
An unusual name coming from the Latin for 'lion'.

Leonard: *Len, Lenny*
From the German for 'bold lion', this name has been in regular, if infrequent, use since the Middle Ages.

Leopold
This name had a brief period of popularity at the time of Queen Victoria as it was the name of some members of the royal family. Originally it came from the German for 'brave people'.

Liopold: *Leo, Lepp*
From the Old German meaning 'brave people'.

Leslie

Leslie has been used as a Christian name only in the last century. Previous to that it was a surname in Scotland, taken from a place-name and meaning 'little meadow'.

Lester

Originally a surname, Lester means 'a man from Leicester'.

Lewis: *Lew, Lou, Louis*

The Normans introduced the name Louis into England. Coming from Old German, it means 'brave warrior'. Lewis is the anglicised version of the name.

Liam

The Irish equivalent of William, meaning 'helmet'.

Lionel

French for 'little lion', this was a popular name in the sixteenth and seventeenth centuries in the north of England.

Llewellyn: *Llew, Llywelyn, Lyn*

Meaning 'young lion', this Celtic name is a favourite in Wales.

Lloyd

A popular Welsh name meaning 'grey'.

Lucas

This is the more unusual version of Luke.

Lucian

An old Syrian name used occasionally in this country.

Ludovic: *Ludovick*

In the last three hundred years Lodovick has been a well-known Scottish name. Ludovick is the English version. It comes from the same origin as Lewis.

Luke

A Greek name which means 'a man from Luciania', it was Saint Luke who influenced the popularity of this name. Many surnames have developed from it, such as Lucas, Luckett and Lucock.

Luther

A German name deriving from a surname, Luther means 'famous warrior'.

Lyndon: *Lindon*

'One who dwells by the lime tree' is the meaning of this Old English name, which does not enjoy much popularity at present.

M

Madoc: *Maddoc*
Meaning 'fortunate', this is a common Welsh name.

Magnus
The Latin word for 'great' was taken as a Christian name originally in Scandinavia. Use of Magnus spread to Scotland, Shetland and Ireland but it has been used only infrequently in England.

Malcolm
A favourite in Scotland, this name, which is from the Gaelic for 'disciple of Saint Columba', is now quite commonly used in Britain.

Mallory
This is usually considered a surname. It means 'an unlucky man'.

Manfred
The Normans introduced this name into England but it has never been particularly well used. It developed from the German for 'peaceful man'.

Manuel
This is the Spanish derivation from Emmanuel, meaning 'God at our side'.

Marius
A name coming from the Latin for 'belonging to the God Mars'.

Mark: *Marc, Marcus*
Marcus was the original name, which was the Latin for the god Mars, god of war. Mark, the anglicised version, has only recently become popular in spite of being the name of the author of one of the Gospels. It is sometimes spelt Marc.

Marlon
A modern name used more often in America, it comes from the French for 'little hawk'.

Martin
This is another derivative of the Latin for 'Mars'. A fourth-century Saint Martin, who was Bishop of Tours, enjoyed great popularity in France and England, and many English churches are dedicated to him. A well-known name at present, it was also particularly popular from the twelfth to the fifteenth century. It is often used as a surname in such forms as Martins, Martinson and Martel.

Marvin
The Old English for 'famous friend' is the basis of this name.

Matthew: *Mat, Matthias*
Originally from the Hebrew for 'God's gift', it was the Normans who brought the name Matthew to England. It was popular in the twelfth, thirteenth and fourteenth centuries and led to the development of a

great many surnames—Macey, Mayhew, Mathewson, Maykin and Matterson being just a few of them. Matthias was a variation of the same name, used by translators of the Bible and consequently an alternative Christian name.

Maurice: *Morris*

Used since the twelfth century, this name came from the Latin for 'a moor'. It used to be spelt Morris but nowadays Maurice is the more usual spelling. It is the basis of such surnames as Morris, Morrison, Morse and Morcock.

Max: *Maximilian*

From the Latin for 'the greatest', Max is the popular version of Maximilian, a name invented in the nineteenth century by the Emperor Frederick III.

Maxwell: *Max*

Until recently this has been just a surname coming from the Old English for 'a large spring'. As a Christian name it is often abbreviated to Max.

Maynard

This is a name, brought to England by the Normans, that came originally from the German for 'tough and strong'.

Melville

More commonly known as a surname, Melville is now used as a Christian name, particularly in America.

Melvin

This name, which is better known in America, probably comes from the Old English for 'chief'.

Meridith: *Meredith*

Meaning 'sea lord', Meridith is a Welsh surname often also given as a first name.

Mervyn: *Mervin*

Another Welsh name, popular not only in Wales but also in northern England in the Middle Ages, Mervyn was the basis of several surnames such as Marvin, Mervin and Murfin.

Michael: *Mick, Mickey, Micky, Mike*

Michael is a favourite English name, with several well-known diminutives. Originally from the Hebrew for 'who is like God', this was the name of one of the archangels to whom many churches have been dedicated since the twelfth century. Michael formed the basis of numerous family names such as Mitchell, Mitchison and Myhill, which are closer to the former pronounciation of the name. In the last three hundred years Michael has come to be the most common given name in Ireland.

Miles

The Normans brought this name to England, where it took hold and led to the development of such surnames as Miles, Milson and Mills.

The name may go back to the sixth century B.C. to the time of the Greek athlete, Milo of Croton, who won the wrestling at both the Olympic and Pythian games six times. At present it is quite well known.

Montague: *Monte, Monty*
A name coming from the French, meaning 'from the pointed hill'.

Morgan
A Gaelic name meaning 'sea dweller'. It is particularly popular in Wales.

Murdoch
Murdoch is less often used now as a first name. It comes from the Celtic for 'man of the sea'.

Murray
This is a surname sometimes used now as a given name. It has the same origins as Murdoch, and means 'sea warrior'.

Mylor
An unusual Christian name coming from the Gaelic for 'prince'.

N

Nathan: *Nat, Natty*
This name is mainly used in Jewish families. It comes from the Hebrew for 'a gift'.

Nathaniel: *Nat*
Hebrew for 'God's gift', Nathaniel is a name that has been used regularly since the Reformation.

Neal: *Neil, Neill*
All three spellings of this name are commonly used at present. Meaning 'champion' in Irish, Neal formed the basis of such family names as Nelson and Nielson.

Nelson
Originally a surname derived from Neal, Nelson has recently been used as a first name, more so in America than here.

Neville
From the French 'neuville', meaning 'newtown', this was a Norman surname that has appeared as a Christian name since the seventeenth century.

Newell
Newell comes form the Latin for 'a kernel'.

Nicholas: *Nick*
Originally from the Greek for 'victory for the people', this was the name of a fourth-century Bishop of Myra in Lycia, who became the patron saint of Russia and Greece and also of sailors, merchants and

children. Saint Nicholas, in the guise of Santa Claus, is the legendary friend of children who brings presents on Christmas eve, or in some European countries on 6 December, which is Saint Nicholas' Day. A common name since before the Norman Conquest, a great many surnames have derived from Nicholas, such as Nicolson, Nixon, Cole and Collins.

Nigel
From the Celtic for 'champion', Nigel came from the same roots as Neil via Scandinavia.

Noah
A Hebrew name meaning 'long lived' that is used occasionally, more often in America.

Noel: *Nowell*
From the French for Christmas, this name was bestowed on children born on Christmas day. It was popular in the Middle Ages and has been used from time to time since then. The anglicised version, Nowell, is sometimes used.

Norbert
A Teutonic name meaning the 'brightness of Niord'.

Norman
From the Old English for 'north man', this was a common English name until the fourteenth century, since when it has been chosen more often in Scotland.

O

Oakley
An unusual first name, taken from the surname and meaning 'field of oak trees'.

Oliver: *Ollie*
Oliver was a well-used Christian name in England from medieval times until the demise of Oliver Cromwell, when it became distinctly unfashionable. In the last hundred years it has become more acceptable as associations with past history have faded. It may have derived from the Latin for 'olive tree' or alternatively may have been used to represent a Teutonic name meaning 'elf host'.

Omar
Meaning 'a shipbuilder', this Arabic name became known in this country because of Edward FitzGerald's translation of the 'Rubáiyát of Omar Khayyám' in 1859. The name is probably more associated now with the actor Omar Sharif.

Orlando
This is the Italian version of Roland, which comes from the Old German for 'fame'.

Ormond: *Ordmund*
Old English in origin, Ormond is an unusual name meaning 'spear-protector' or 'ship protector'.

Orson
An uncommon name that comes from the Latin for 'a bear cub'.

Osbert
From the Old English for 'bright god', this is an old Northumbrian name that faded from popularity but which has been used again recently.

Osborn
Although better known as a surname now, this used to be an Old English Christian name, meaning 'god's man', that was popular both before and after the Norman Conquest.

Oscar
Another Anglo-Saxon name, meaning 'god's spear', Oscar was little used in this country after the Norman invasion although it does appear in Ireland. It has recently been revived.

Osmond: *Osmund*
Meaning 'god's protection' in Old English, Osmond continued in use for a couple of centuries after 1066. Since then it has generally been used as a surname in its various spellings.

Oswald
This name has never gone out of favour since its first use in the eleventh century. It comes from the Old English for 'divine power'.

Otis
Otis is more commonly used in America. It is of Greek origin and means 'acute hearing'.

Otto
An old Teutonic name meaning 'rich' was the basis of this modern German name, which is now used sometimes in Britain.

Owen
A very popular name in Wales, Owen comes from the Celtic for 'well born'.

P

Pascoe: *Pascal*
This name comes from the Latin for 'Easter'. Pascoe is better known as a surname except perhaps in the Cornwall area.

Patrick: *Pat, Paddy*
From the Latin for 'nobleman', this was the name taken by Ireland's apostle. It is a popular choice in that country and to a lesser extent in northern England and Scotland.

Paul
Although this is a favourite name at the present time it has not been widely used in the past in spite of the well-known biblical story of Saint Paul. It comes from the Latin for 'little'. Paulin, Pawley and Powell are surnames which have derived from it.

Percival
From the French for 'pierce the valley', Percival has been used occasionally as a Christian name since the thirteenth century. As a surname it has been in use even longer.

Percy
Originally a French village name in Normandy, this was the name of one of William the Conqueror's companions. Use of the name outside the family was unusual until the nineteenth century, when it became relatively common.

Peregrine: *Perry*
An unusual name from the Latin for 'a traveller'. There was a seventh-century Saint Peregrinus who was a hermit near Modena.

Peter: *Pete*
From the Greek for 'a rock', this was the name Jesus gave to Simon, son of Jonas. It was introduced into England by the Normans and became extremely popular, Saint Peter having more churches dedicated to him than to any other saint. After the Reformation the name fell from fashion, but in this century it has again become a favourite.

Philip: *Phillip*
Another Apostle's name Philip, has never fallen from favour since the Middle Ages. It has given rise to many surnames, such as Phillips, Phelps. Philcox and Phipps. It comes from the Greek for 'lover of horses'.

Piers: *Pierre*
Piers is the original French version of Peter whilst Pierre is the modern form.

Pugh
This is a Welsh name meaning 'son of Hu'.

Q

Quentin: *Quintin*
From the Latin for 'fifth', Quentin was introduced by the Normans. In France it was a popular choice around the area where a third-century Saint Quentin had been martyred.

Quin: *Quinn*
A Celtic name that means 'the wise'. It is not in vogue at present.

Quincey
'One who dwells at the home of the fifth son' is the meaning of Quincey, which is not a popular first name. It is occasionally heard as a surname.

R

Ralph: *Rafe, Ralf*
Ralf is an Old English name meaning 'wolf's counsel' that has been in use since before the Norman invasion. Rafe is a modern phonetic spelling that in fact reflects the former pronunciation of Ralph.

Randal: *Randall*
Meaning 'wolf's shield', this is an Anglo-Saxon name that survived after 1066. It is more common as a surname now, although some gypsy families still choose to give it to their children.

Randolph
This is an eighteenth-century variant of Randal.

Raoul
This is really the French form of Ralph, which was well known in England in the Middle Ages when French was still spoken. It formed the basis of such family names as Rawlings and Rawlinson. A few children were christened Raoul after the First World War when soldiers serving in France again took a fancy to the name.

Raphael
From the Hebrew for 'God's healing', this was the name of one of the archangels. Although not common now, it was quite often chosen in the sixteenth and seventeenth centuries.

Raymond: *Ray, Raymund*
It was the Normans who brought this name to England. It comes originally from the Old German for 'strong protection', Ray is the diminutive form, which is sometimes used now as a separate name.

Redmond
This is a Teutonic name meaning 'protection by the counsellors'.

Reginald: *Reg, Reggie, Rex*
This name, which was revived in the nineteenth century, dates back to before the Norman Conquest. It comes from the Old English for 'mighty strength'. Some surnames that developed from it are Reynolds, Reynoldson and Rennell.

René
Unusual although not unknown in this country, René is a French name that comes from the Latin for 'reborn'. In the fifth century there was a Saint René who was Bishop of Angers.

Reuben
Reuben is a Hebrew name given to a boy taking the place of a dead son. It has been used in this country during the last three hundred years.

Rex
This is a modern Christian name taken from the Latin for 'king'. It is sometimes used as a familiar form of Reginald.

Rhys
A favourite Welsh name meaning 'impetuous man'.

Richard: *Dick, Rich, Rick, Ritchie*
One of the most common boys' names, this meant 'stern ruler' in Old English. It was the Normans who led to the rise in popularity of Richard, which was also a French name. Ritchie is the more common diminutive in America and Scotland, whereas Rick, Rich and Dick are more usual in England.

Robert: *Bob, Bobby, Rab, Rabbie, Rob*
An Old English name meaning 'bright fame' that was also used by the Normans, Robert has never fallen from favour. There have been many nicknames derived from it, those in use at the moment being Bob and Rob in England and Rab and Rabbie in Scotland. Several surnames have also stemmed from Robert, such as Robertson, Robins, Robeson, Hobbs, Hopkins and Dobson.

Robin
This name, which is now used independently, is a derivative of Robert.

Roderick: *Rod, Roddy, Roderic*
Roderick is a name more commonly used in Scotland than in the rest of Britain. It comes from the Old German for 'famous ruler'.

Rodney: *Rod, Roddy*
The use of Rodney as a Christian name dates back to the famous eighteenth century Admiral Lord Rodney. Previous to that time it was a surname peculiar to the Avon area in England.

Roger: *Rodger, Rog*
Hrothgar, an Old English name meaning 'spear fame', was reinforced with the French Roger. It came to be one of the most frequently used names in the Middle Ages and forms the basis of such surnames as

Rodgers, Dodge, Hodgkins and Hotchkiss. After a couple of centuries of disuse it is again a favourite choice.

Roland: *Rollo, Roly, Rowland*
A French name meaning 'famous in the land', popularised by the epic poem 'La Chanson de Roland', which tells of the heroic death of one of Charlemagne's noblemen, Roland was brought to England by the Normans. It was frequently used in the Middle Ages and has been in regular if occasional use since then.

Rolf: *Rolfe, Rollo, Rolph*
Originating from the Old German for 'famous wolf', this was another name introduced by the Normans. After a while its popularity waned but recently it has started to be used again.

Ronald: *Ron*
Ronald is the Scottish equivalent of Reginald, but in recent times it has also been used in England.

Rory: *Rorie*
This comes from the Gaelic for 'red' or 'ruddy'.

Roscoe
Until recently Roscoe was just a surname but it is now being used as a first name. Its meaning is 'from the roe-deer forest'.

Ross
An unusual name, Ross comes from the Gaelic for 'dweller at the promontory'. It is also a surname.

Roy
From the Celtic for 'red', this is a Scottish name now used on both sides of the border.

Royston
This name, which became popular in the 1930s, used to be a surname taken from a Yorkshire place-name.

Rudolf
Rudolf is a modern German name meaning 'wolf' that is sometimes chosen here.

Rudyard
Made popular by Rudyard Kipling, this unusual Old English name means 'from the red enclosure'. It is rarely used as a Christian name today.

Rufus
Rufus comes from the Latin for 'red-haired'.

Rupert
This is a German name coming from the same root as Robert and meaning 'bright fame'.

Russell: *Russ, Rusty*
Russell comes from the Old French for 'red head'.

S

Samson: *Sam, Sampson*
This name of the famous biblical warrior comes from the Hebrew for 'sun child'.

Samuel: *Sam, Sammy*
Samuel is Hebrew for 'name of God'. The Puritans used it to translate an old Norse name meaning 'summer wanderer' and it came to be a favourite choice in the seventeenth century.

Sanders: *Saunders*
These are both Scottish derivatives of Alexander.

Sandy
This is a modern innovation that is a further diminutive of Alexander.

Saul
Saul was the name of the first king of Israel. It comes from the Hebrew for 'asked for'.

Scott
Originally a surname, Scott is Old English for 'from Scotland'. Of late, it is increasing in popularity.

Seamus: *Seumus, Shamus*
Seumus, the Irish form of James, is often spelt inaccurately as Seamus. The name has been anglicised as Shamus.

Sean: *Shane, Shaun*
John in Ireland becomes Sean and this name in turn becomes Shaun in England and Shane in America.

Sebastian: *Seb*
Meaning 'venerated' in Latin, Sebastian was the name of a martyr put to death by being shot by arrows in the third century.

Selwyn
Selwyn is an Old English name meaning 'house friend' and is now quite common in Wales.

Seth
Seth, the name of one of Adam's sons born after Abel died, became popular in the mid nineteenth century. It comes from the Hebrew for 'the chosen one'.

Shaw
This name, which is known more as a surname than a Christian name, means 'dweller at a grove of trees' in Old English.

Shelley
Shelley, another first name taken from a surname, is Old English for 'wood or clearing on a bank'.

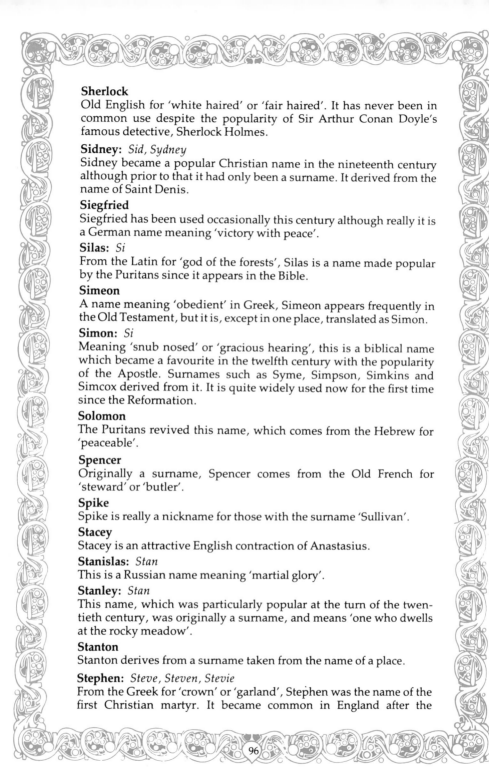

Sherlock

Old English for 'white haired' or 'fair haired'. It has never been in common use despite the popularity of Sir Arthur Conan Doyle's famous detective, Sherlock Holmes.

Sidney: *Sid, Sydney*

Sidney became a popular Christian name in the nineteenth century although prior to that it had only been a surname. It derived from the name of Saint Denis.

Siegfried

Siegfried has been used occasionally this century although really it is a German name meaning 'victory with peace'.

Silas: *Si*

From the Latin for 'god of the forests', Silas is a name made popular by the Puritans since it appears in the Bible.

Simeon

A name meaning 'obedient' in Greek, Simeon appears frequently in the Old Testament, but it is, except in one place, translated as Simon.

Simon: *Si*

Meaning 'snub nosed' or 'gracious hearing', this is a biblical name which became a favourite in the twelfth century with the popularity of the Apostle. Surnames such as Syme, Simpson, Simkins and Simcox derived from it. It is quite widely used now for the first time since the Reformation.

Solomon

The Puritans revived this name, which comes from the Hebrew for 'peaceable'.

Spencer

Originally a surname, Spencer comes from the Old French for 'steward' or 'butler'.

Spike

Spike is really a nickname for those with the surname 'Sullivan'.

Stacey

Stacey is an attractive English contraction of Anastasius.

Stanislas: *Stan*

This is a Russian name meaning 'martial glory'.

Stanley: *Stan*

This name, which was particularly popular at the turn of the twentieth century, was originally a surname, and means 'one who dwells at the rocky meadow'.

Stanton

Stanton derives from a surname taken from the name of a place.

Stephen: *Steve, Steven, Stevie*

From the Greek for 'crown' or 'garland', Stephen was the name of the first Christian martyr. It became common in England after the

Norman invasion and led to the development of such surnames as Stevens, Stephenson and Stenson.

Sterling
This is a name with Teutonic origins meaning 'good value'.

Stewart: *Stuart*
Stewart was originally a surname coming from the Old English for a 'steward'. As a Christian name it has been used since the middle of the nineteenth century.

Sullivan
Usually known as a surname, Sullivan means 'hawk-eye' or 'black eye'.

Sylvester: *Silvester*
In the Middle Ages Sylvester was quite a common Christian name. It was taken from the name of the Roman god 'Silvanus', who was god of fields and forests. A Saint Silvester was reputed to have cured the Emperor Constantine of his leprosy.

T

Taffy
This is a Welsh diminutive of David.

Tam: *Tammie*
In Scotland these are the familiar forms of Thomas.

Ted: *Teddy*
Both the names Edward and occasionally Theodore are abbreviated to Ted or Teddy.

Terence: *Terry*
This comes from the Latin name Terentius, which was the name of a humanitarian dramatist whose plays were based on Greek comedies. Terence was particularly popular in the middle of the twentieth century.

Theobald: *Theo*
Theobald is a Teutonic name meaning 'bold people' that has been used in Britain since before the Norman Conquest.

Theodore
A Greek name meaning 'divine gift', Theodore was the name of a seventh-century Archbishop of Canterbury after whom many people named their children. In America it is often abbreviated to Teddy.

Therron
Therron comes from the Greek for 'hunter'.

Thomas: *Tom, Tommy*
Meaning 'a twin' in Aramaic, this has been one of the more popular

boys' names in England since the Norman invasion. Before then it had only been a priest's name. It was probably Saint Thomas of Canterbury, murdered in the twelfth century, who led to the name being such a popular choice. Tomlinson, Toms and Tomkins are some of the surnames that have developed from it.

Thurstan
This is a Danish name meaning 'stone of the God Thor'.

Timothy: *Tim, Timbo, Timmie*
Meaning 'honoured by God' in Greek, this is a biblical name that began to be used after the Reformation.

Titus
This name has been used occasionally in Britain during the last three hundred years. It is mentioned in the Bible as being that of one of Saint Paul's disciples.

Toby: *Tobias*
The name Tobias derived from the Hebrew for 'God is good'. Toby is the anglicised version, which is very fashionable at present.

Tony: *Tone*
These are both diminutives of Antony, Tony now being accepted as a distinct name.

Trevor: *Trev*
From a Welsh surname meaning 'big village', Trevor is now used as a Christian name.

Tristram: *Tristan*
From the Celtic for 'tumult', this name is probably best known in connection with the legend of 'Tristan and Isolde'.

U

Ulric
Ulric comes from the Anglo-Saxon for 'wolf ruler'.

Ulysses
This name, which has been used in Ireland, is the Latin for the Greek hero Odysseus.

Urian
Urian is a Welsh name meaning 'born in a town'.

V

Valentine
Valentine is a Latin name meaning 'robust and healthy'.

Valerian
This name has been more widely used in France than in this country because there was a Saint Valerianus of Auxerre. It comes from the Latin for 'strong'.

Vance
Vance has until recently been considered a surname, associated with the harvest as it means 'a thresher'.

Vaughn: *Vaughan*
'Little man' in Celtic was the basis of this name, which has been used as a Christian name for only a short while.

Vere
This was a surname meaning 'from Ver', which is a place-name in France. It is now used as a first name.

Vernon
A surname originating from a place-name in France and meaning 'elder tree', Vernon has been used as a fore-name since the nineteenth century.

Victor: *Vic*
From the Latin for 'a conqueror', Victor was unusual as a Christian name until the second part of the nineteenth century, when it was probably used because of its similarity with the queen's name.

Vincent: *Vince*
This name, which was quite well known in this country in the nineteenth century, means 'conquering' in Latin. It was the name of a third-century martyr from Saragossa in Spain whose influence was widespread.

Virgil
Virgil comes from the Latin for 'to flourish'.

Vivian
From the Latin for 'alive' or 'lively', this name has been used inter-mittently since the twelfth century.

W

Wade
Wade is an Old English name meaning 'the advancer'.

Waldo
This is Old German for 'power'. It is not in common use as a Christian name.

Wallace: *Wallis, Wally*
Recently taken up as a Christian name, Wallace was the surname of a Scottish hero. It is both a boy's and girl's name, and is Old English for 'Welsh man or woman'.

Walter: *Wally, Walt, Wat, Wattie*
From the German for 'folk ruler', this was a popular name with the Normans, who introduced it into England. It has been in regular use since then and has given rise to such surnames as Waterson, Watkins and Watts.

Warner
This name, which is more popular in America than here, comes from an Old German folk-name.

Warren
From the German folk-name Varin, Warren was brought to England by the Normans and used for a couple of centuries before dropping from favour. Taken from the current surname, Warren has again been in use as a first name in this country.

Wayne
Wayne comes from the Old English for 'wagoner' or 'wagon maker' and is both a surname and a Christian name.

Wilfrid: *Wilf, Wilfred*
Saint Wilfrith, who was Bishop of York, was a prominent personage in the seventh century. His name was little used after the Norman Conquest but again became popular in the nineteenth century. It comes from the Old English for 'hope for peace'.

William: *Bill, Billy, Will, Willie, Willy*
William comes from the German for 'helmet of strong resolution' and it was the Normans who brought the name to England. It has been popular ever since and many surnames have developed from its use, such as Wilson, Wilcox, Wilkinson and Williams.

Wilmer
A Teutonic name meaning 'willing warrior'.

Wilmot
This is an unusual variant of William.

Winston
This was a place-name that has been used in the Churchill family since the seventeenth century as a first name.

Wystan
Wystan comes from the Old English for 'battle stone' and was the name of a ninth-century boy king murdered in his youth and later venerated as a saint, particularly in the Midlands.

X

Xavier: *Savy*
This is a Spanish name made popular by Saint Francis Xavier in the sixteenth century. He was a Jesuit missionary, who with Saint Ignatius Loyola founded the Society of Jesus. He travelled a great deal in the Far East and was called the Apostle of the Indies.

Y

Yorick
This name, which Shakespeare used in *Hamlet*, is probably based on a phonetic spelling of the Danish version of George.

Z

Zachary: *Zack, Zacky*
From the Hebrew for 'God remembered', Zacharias was the name both of a prophet and of an Israelite king. Simplified as Zachary, the name was often used in the seventeenth century and has continued in use since then.

Zane
This is an unusual variant of John.

Zebedee
Zebedee is of doubtful origin but may come from the Hebrew for 'father'.

Zenon
Zenon comes from the Greek for 'from the God Zeus'.

INTRODUCTION

Every child has a personality from birth. This can be affected by circumstances, and encouraged or thwarted by parental influence — but innate character is retained throughout life.

I believe that clues to this character lie in the ancient art of astrology. According to his or her month of birth, the child will develop according to the traditional Zodiacal patterns. This is not simply hearsay or superstition; nowadays there is practical proof that character is somehow governed by the position of the sun at birth.

According to the medieval 'law of correspondences', there were, on the one hand, a multitude of links between Zodiac signs and planets, and, on the other, many different aspects of life — from precious stones, flowers, plants, colours, in fact everything under the sun.

Some of these old ideas are fairly whimsical, but others seem to be based on a true, if still mysterious, understanding of nature. Recent metallurgical research, for instance, has shown that the metals given under each sign do undergo chemical changes when the celestial influences are at work. From my own experience, too, I have noticed that gardeners born under a particular sign seem to have green fingers as far as 'their' plants and flowers are concerned.

There are twelve problem areas in the Zodiac: the so-called cusps between one sign and the next. People born in these 'grey' areas are never sure which sign they belong to; and in their personalities they sometimes seem to veer from one set of characteristics to the next. The cuspal area is usually the last two days of each sign; but because the precise Zodiac dates do vary fractionally from year to year, a cuspal baby should have his or her precise horoscope calculated.

Real astrology goes into the subject much more deeply, of course. From the complete map of the sky at birth — known as the horoscope — it is possible to glean a remarkably detailed portrait of the child: outer temperament, inner emotional disposition, aptitudes and talents and ability — or otherwise — to get on well with others.

Through my organization, Starlife, it is possible for you to get a completely personal report on your child. If you would like further details of this service, write to:

Roger Elliot, Starlife, Cossington, Bridgewater, Somerset

Roger Elliot

Signs of the zodiac

ARIES

(March 21st to April 20th)

Those born under Aries are strong and independent people with a firm grip on reality. They grow into self-reliant adults, sometimes a bit tactless but always full of enterprise.

Aries babies are often quick to walk, talk and make their presence felt. Their natural courage makes them dare-devils — dangerously so until they have been taught commonsense. A family knows when there's an Aries baby about!

Besides commonsense, they need to be taught kindness and perhaps generosity. Little Aries children are not malicious, but they do not always realise the harm they do when pulling off the butterfly's wings! Nor are they naturally greedy — but they do think of their own needs first, and should be taught how to put other people first.

Aries children are meant to be competitive, but often they will only compete when they know they are going to win! On the whole, they are sociable people, able to mix with a wide variety of adults and other children. But they must be taught co-operation with others, and how to take a back seat at times. Aries boys always want to be centre-forward, never the goalie!

Aries girls are natural tomboys. All Aries children have strength. They like tackling new projects, going to new places and making a big impression. They are not academic by nature, preferring sport to study, and often choose careers with a breath of fresh air involved: sports coaches, farmers, geologists or engineers.

In their development a lot depends on Dad. It is his example which has a lasting impression on the Aries child.

ARIES

Colours: bright primary colours, particularly scarlet and yellow. Red is the colour of Mars, ruler of Aries.

Stones: diamonds, garnets and bloodstones.

Metals: iron and steel.

Trees: all thorn-bearing trees and shrubs.

Flowers: daffodils, tulips, honeysuckle.

Countries: England, France, Germany, Poland.

Cities: Naples, Florence, Birmingham.

TAURUS

(April 21st to May 21st)

Taureans are the most down-to-earth people in the Zodiac. They are the great constructors — the ones who need to build a career, a home and family, a lifestyle that will last a lifetime.

As a result, Taurus babies take their time — but once they have found their feet they become sturdy toddlers. You cannot expect them to be precocious; they do everything carefully, thoughtfully — but once a habit is learnt, it lasts forever.

On the whole they're happy and friendly children, well able to mix with others. But they can be stubborn at times. When they do dig in their heels, the only way to relax them is smiles and kindness, for they are very loving creatures who do not enjoy being a trouble.

From an early age they need to develop their constructive skills. Both boys and girls will enjoy tackling household and garden chores, and love playing with tools. They have a built-in sense of values and should be encouraged to treasure beautiful and valuable belongings. They will also enjoy having their own pocket-money and need to be taught sensible budgeting from an early age.

All their lives they will be hospitable people. As children they should be allowed to give their own parties, for instance, and be encouraged to decorate their rooms in their own way. But they are not terribly adventurous by nature. Taureans are rarely leaders of the pack, they prefer to be steady second-in-commands. It's important that they don't fall behind in their studies through lack of praise at home.

They are great family people. So long as they have a happy home, they'll develop into warm and generous adults.

TAURUS

Colours: cream, madonna blue, spring green. Blue is
the colour of Venus, ruler of Taurus.

Stones: emeralds, coral and lapis lazuli.

Metal: copper.

Trees: ash, cypress and apple.

Flowers: rose, poppy, violets and foxgloves.

Countries: Cyprus, Eire and Iran.

Cities: Dublin, Leipzig and St Louis, Miss.

GEMINI

(May 22nd to June 21st)

All Geminians are Peter Pans at heart. They are natural children right through their lives, and their biggest problem is learning how to grow up.

You can expect them to talk early — and to continue talking non-stop! They are the world's great chatterers, which can be infuriating at times — but remember that their verbal dexterity is a wonderful gift. They should be encouraged to do drama from an early age and to express themselves on the written page.

They are probably the friendliest creatures in the Zodiac, making acquaintances left, right and centre. But you'll find that they do not form deep friendships and they will work through a succession of 'best friends', dropping them abruptly at a moment's notice.

This inconsistency is perhaps their worst fault. It will come out in their schoolwork, too. With subjects they enjoy, such as English and mathematics, they'll do well — but with other subjects they'll cheat and muddle their way through! Gemini children are little liars. If they think they can get away with it, they'll fib and pretend and make things up, sometimes out of devilment, often because they talk themselves into it. So they must be taught the virtues of steady endeavour . . . and honesty.

Sometimes their health is suspect in the early years. Take special care of them during bronchial troubles. They are nervous children, full of vitality but rarely wanting to accept responsibility for their actions. It's terribly easy to spoil them, because they have so much gamin charm. But in the end they must be encouraged to grow up!

GEMINI

Colours: saffron yellow, and black and white contrasts. The colour of Mercury, ruler of Gemini, is white.

Stones: crystal, topaz and beryl.

Metal: mercury.

Trees: nut-trees, rowans and beech.

Flowers: lily-of-the-valley, lavender and rock-roses.

Countries: Wales, America and Belgium.

Cities: London, Melbourne and San Francisco.

CANCER

(June 22nd to July 22nd)

Those born under Cancer are like their symbol, the crab — tough on the outside, but sensitive underneath. They put on a brave show, but inwardly they're shy and soft.

They are moody creatures, full of excitement one moment and depressed the next. As infants they can veer from docility to tantrums and back again. They take their food seriously, probably benefit more from the breast than the bottle, and need, above all, a stable and loving family background.

Mother is the most important person in any Cancerian's young life. She will have an indelible effect on their development, for better or worse. This becomes crucial in the case of boys; for if they are over-protected by Mum, they could remain mother's boys for the whole of their lives. It's vital that she unties the apron-strings.

All Cancer children are shy at first, but soon make warm, close friendships. They know who 'belongs' and who is a stranger. If you can win their hearts, they are yours for life, for they radiate a fiercely possessive affection.

At school they do well in English, history and sometimes languages, but less brilliantly in science subjects. They nearly always have artistic aptitude and love being in school plays. It is their imagination that should be kindled from their earliest years; the grown-up who will tell them stories is performing the best service possible.

It's hard for a Cancerian to be straightforward and blunt. Like the crab, they edge sideways all the time. They are born cowards, and dislike the rough-and-tumble of the playground. But in their own ways they are sweet, adorable children.

CANCER

Colours: silver, cerulean blue and sea-green. Silver and smoky grey are the colours of the Moon, ruler of Cancer.

Stones: pearl and moonstone.

Metal: silver.

Trees: willow, spruce and pear trees.

Flowers: daisy, acanthus and iris.

Countries: Holland, Paraguay and Scotland.

Cities: Manchester, Amsterdam and New York.

LEO

(July 23rd to August 23rd)

Most people are children for only the first fifteen years of life, but Leo types like to think of themselves as children all their lives! At their best, they have an innocent, wholehearted approach to life without a note of cynicism.

As babies they should beam with health and happiness, though, just as the sun can be obscured by a single cloud, so can the bonny Leo sunshine suddenly turn into despair if something goes wrong.

Leo children want to be surrounded by love and affection, and adore being flattered; but it's a mistake to spoil them too much — for once they are indulged, they never lose a taste for it. They must be brought up to accept that other people — brothers and sisters in particular — need love as much as they do, so there should be no reason for jealousy.

All Leo children like the opportunity to take charge and stand in the spotlight. Fancy-dress parties are a favourite amusement, for they love being noticed. In a group of children, the Leonian will soon stand out, provided he is genuinely popular. He or she can only command through personal charisma; and if this is lacking, they can become sulky.

At school they do well in sports, drama, initiative tests and art, but they do not necessarily have a scientific frame of mind. They prefer to leave detailed work to others, so they must be trained to be consistent and accurate.

At worst, Leo kids are proud, bumptious and horribly vain. At best, they radiate such joy and warmth that they are a delight to have near you.

LEO

Colours: gold, gold and gold!

Stones: ruby, diamond and hyacinth.

Metal: gold, of course!

Trees: palm, citrus fruit trees and rhododendron.

Flowers: sunflower, potentilla and many annuals.

Countries: France, Italy and Syria.

Cities: Rome, Bombay and Philadelphia.

VIRGO

(August 24th to September 22nd)

Virgoans are often called the salt of the earth. Salt is very useful in cooking, but has not great personality itself; and in some ways this is true of Virgo, too. Children born under this Zodiac sign have many virtues, but they rarely have great zest or bonhomie. They are more subdued than that.

As babies they can be nervous and fussy about food, and seem more prone to little ailments than do other infants. But they often talk early, and can be highly inquisitive toddlers. They have a natural aptitude for mechanical objects and love to discover for themselves how things work.

Because they are not natural extroverts, they do not go out and make friends; instead, they allow chance meetings gradually to grow into personal relationships. Their shyness is not inhibition so much as modesty; but once friends are made, they will last a long time.

In personal behaviour, the Virgo child is usually neat, tidy and efficient. At school, he or she can do well in a wide variety of subjects, for Virgo is a naturally academic Zodiac sign. There should be special aptitude in mathematics, drawing and languages. Sport and physical exercise are not so popular.

Virgo children want to serve others. They will take an early delight in helping their mother around the house and later will love to join worthwhile groups like the Scouts, Guides or local charities. At school, too, they love to keep the wheels smoothly turning, and frequently become 'teacher's pets'.

They are choosy people, which makes them finicky at times. They need warmth, admiration and sensible ambitions to work for.

VIRGO

Colours: light blue and pure white, and pastel colours in neat patterns. White is the colour of Mercury, ruler of Virgo.

Stones: pink jasper, hyacinth and topaz.

Metal: platinum.

Trees: cherry, cotoneaster and birch.

Flowers: alpines, rock plants and autumn bulbs.

Countries: Brazil, Turkey and Switzerland.

Cities: Los Angeles, Paris and Jerusalem.

LIBRA

(September 23rd to October 23rd)

Librans are the dainty members of the Zodiac. They have great taste and discrimination and prefer to spend their lives in as gentle and harmonious an environment as possible. Not always is this possible; and through their family upbringing they are taught to make the best of sometimes difficult circumstances.

As babies they are soft, cuddly and generally passive. They can't be hurried into walking and talking, though they are greatly helped by older brothers and sisters. Their nickname is 'Lazy Libra', which seems true of them from the earliest age! Don't expect them to work hard; they're the greatest armchair experts in the world!

They are also the greatest mixers. So long as they feel a gentle rapport coming their way, they adore meeting new people and making new friends. As young children they will enjoy playing with girls more than boys, as they dislike the aggression and competitiveness of tough male company. But once they reach the teenage years, Librans enjoy mixing with the opposite sex. Libran youths become ladies' men, while Libran young ladies like to feel cherished by boy-friends.

All their lives they will be dithery, scared of making irrevocable decisions. This makes it hard for them to choose a definite career or even to have a clear-cut ambition in mind. True, they are willing to take other people's advice; but if the advice is poor, they end up as losers.

They are much influenced by other children around them. No Libran likes to be an only child, and it's important that they mix with the right friendly crowd from an early age.

LIBRA

Colours: pale greens, pretty pinks and all pastel shades. Clear blue is the colour of Venus, ruler of Libra.

Stones: diamond, cornelian and lapis lazuli.

Metal: copper and aluminium.

Trees: acer, laburnum and plum trees.

Flowers: cyclamen, clematis and biennials.

Countries: Austria, Burma and Japan.

Cities: Leeds, Vienna and Johannesburg.

SCORPIO

(October 24th to November 22nd)

Those born under Scorpio are the tough and determined members of the Zodiac. They have a complex, multi-layered personality that can veer from devotion to anger in a split second.

You can tell something about which way the Scorpio child will develop from his behaviour as an infant. If he bawls and screeches, he may well be a rebel all his life. If he's quiet and concentrated, you have the makings of a fine human being.

All Scorpio children have intense feelings which they tend to keep to themselves. This natural secrecy makes them seem difficult at times. They do not mix quite as freely as other children, preferring one very close friend to a wide circle of acquaintances.

They have tremendous will power at their disposal. They should be encouraged to focus on some activity — sport, a school subject, a leisure pursuit — to which they can devote themselves. At heart they want to be winners.

Scorpio children are a problem at times. They can lie without blinking an eyelid; they want power even though they may not deserve it; and occasionally there's a thoughtless cruelty that needs to be checked. On the positive side, they are great self-improvers if given half a chance, and respond magnificently to a fine moral example.

They will prove very good at some subjects and quite indifferent to others, though they are capable of flourishing at almost anything – especially biology, mathematics, physics and chemistry.

To bring up a Scorpio child successfully is one of the most exciting and rewarding achievements known to humankind!

SCORPIO

Colours: dark red, brown and black. These are the colours associated with Pluto, ruler of Scorpio.

Stones: topaz, malachite and jasper.

Metal: sodium.

Trees: yew, cedar and acacia.

Flowers: azalea, gladiolus and hellebore.

Countries: Algeria, Norway and Palestine.

Cities: Liverpool, Washington DC and New Orleans.

SAGITTARIUS

(November 23rd to December 21st)

Sagittarians are the live-wires of the Zodiac. They are born enthusiasts, relishing the idea of a new project to tackle. Ideally they combine this derring-do with responsibility and compassion.

As little children they can be tearaways, crawling and running well before other kids and getting into all kinds of mischief. This inquisitiveness leads to endless cries of 'Why, mummy, why?', for all their lives they will want to combine understanding with discovery.

Socially they are fascinating creatures, liking other children but somehow remaining independent, as all explorers should be! Their ability to argue — and their delight in winning a point — sometimes makes them too aggressive for gentler souls. Much of their upbringing revolves around the need to tame the wild side of their nature. In their hearts they are thoroughly decent people, but over-excitable at times!

Usually they are devoted to sport and other outdoor activities: camping, trekking and the like. Sagittarian girls are natural tomboys and need as open and free an upbringing as possible. Boys and girls are drawn to active, physical careers — perhaps in the armed services, or as travellers, pilots, couriers or whatever. In academic subjects, they are drawn to law, diplomacy and teaching.

Sagittarian children have a disconcerting ability to tell the truth, even when it's embarrassing. They enjoy practical jokes, acting the fool and feeling full of righteous indignation. Their worst faults are a tendency to lose their temper too easily, as well as a desire to show off! They are natural extroverts.

SAGITTARIUS

Colours: warm brown autumnal tints and brilliant blue. Dark blue is the colour of Jupiter, ruler of Sagittarius.

Stones: carbuncle, topaz and hyacinth.

Metal: tin.

Trees: lime, mulberry and oak.

Flowers: asparagus, pinks and carnations.

Countries: Australia, Hungary and Spain.

Cities: Toledo, Cologne and Sheffield.

CAPRICORN

(December 22nd to January 20th)

Capricorn people are often slow developers; it takes time for their true personalities to emerge. They are happier in their middle years than in their youth, but their upbringing can have a crucial effect on their adult lives.

As children, Capricornians can be rather shy and reserved, slowly making a few good friends rather than rushing into a wide circle of acquaintances. If they are slow at walking and talking, don't worry — they like to progress at their own steady pace. All their lives they will be loners to some extent, but that doesn't mean that they don't need a great deal of sensible encouragement. You can't fool Capricorn children; they know the difference between praise and flattery.

They often take after their father and certainly the male parental influence is crucial to their development. From an early age they can accept responsibility. They enjoy being trusted, given practical jobs to tackle around the home, and above all *earning* privileges through good behaviour. They should be allowed to choose how to spend their own pocket-money, and under the right guidance will soon develop a sound financial sense!

This will continue through their schooldays. They are capable of achieving a fine academic record, especially in science, history and mathematics. In adult life, Capricornians may choose teaching, the law, engineering or business as a career.

You can always appeal to a Capricorn's reasonableness – and to his or her sense of duty and moral obligation.

CAPRICORN

Colours: deep green, brown, dark grey. Cool green is the colour of Saturn, ruler of Capricorn.

Stones: white onyx, jet and sapphire.

Metal: lead.

Trees: pine, elm and poplar.

Flowers: pansies, ivy and sedum.

Countries: India, Greece and Mexico.

Cities: Oxford, Brussels and Port Said.

AQUARIUS

(January 21st to February 18th)

Aquarians are the odd ones out in the Zodiac! They cannot be easily pinned down, nor do they conform to a single pattern — for the good reason that they are non-conformists at heart! They like to go their own way.

As infants, they can be over-excitable and are slightly more susceptible to viruses than other children. They are adventurous but not foolhardy, preferring to explore ideas rather than climb trees! You'll notice how observant they are, and often how humorous.

As Aquarian children grow, they make friends easily, but always retain a quality of independence. They like to choose their own friends and can sometimes be rude — or at least forthright — to children that their parents consider 'suitable'. As they approach the teenage years, they can become very rebellious and it's no good trying to fight this attitude. Only an appeal to reason will succeed with a fractious Aquarian child.

They have a keen interest in anything very modern or very ancient: scientific gadgets, archaeology, aircraft and space travel and Stonehenge! They are not likely to be sports-mad and are not notably competitive either. Throughout their lives they try to balance their desire for personal freedom with their willingness to co-operate with others.

Sometimes they will appear to dither when faced by a puzzling choice. They mix as easily with boys as with girls. Always they will be drawn by the idea of foreign travel and it's a good idea to arrange correspondence with a pen pal from another country.

AQUARIUS

Colours: electric blue, shocking pink, fluorescent hues! All the colours of the rainbow are the colours of Uranus, ruler of Aquarius.

Stones: sapphire, opal and chalcedony.

Metal: uranium.

Trees: strawberry tree, cornus and eucalyptus.

Flowers: orchids, pelargonium and hibiscus.

Countries: Sweden, Russia and Ethiopia.

Cities: Bremen, Hamburg and Brighton.

PISCES

(February 19th to March 20th)

Piscean children are soft, sensitive and vulnerable. They need an upbringing that will toughen them up enough to cope with the real world — but not so tough that their tender inner feelings are blotted out.

You will notice their moodiness from the maternity hospital onwards. They will veer high and low according to the weather, the environment around them and, most of all, the mood of the family. All Piscean children are a touch psychic, picking up unspoken thoughts. So they need a stable, loving family background more than most children.

Often they'll seem to live in a dreamworld of their own. Don't worry about this — if anything, encourage their creative imagination by telling stories to them. Any artistic aptitude should be encouraged straight away, but don't expect the Piscean child to persevere. Discipline is not the strongest Piscean virtue.

Certainly, in their dealings with other children, you'll notice that Pisceans can be easily influenced by stronger personalities. This means that they can be led into bad company. It is rather easy for Pisceans to become emotionally fixated — on a habit, a person or a subject.

At school they are drawn to the arts — painting, music and dancing in particular. But they need careful guidance from parents and teachers to ensure that they keep on keeping on — otherwise they will fail to achieve much.

Their worst faults are over-emotionalism (verging on hysterics at times), a lack of courage, and a tendency to escape reality if they can. Their best qualities are a wonderful capacity to love and cherish (they respond to pet animals very sweetly indeed), plus a spiritual awareness that needs developing.

PISCES

Colours: violet, white and blue-grey. Blue is the colour of Jupiter, ruler of Pisces.

Stones: amethyst, chrysolite and topaz.

Metal: tin.

Trees: fig, peaches and malus.

Flowers: water-lilies, delphinium and dahlias.

Countries: Portugal, the Sahara and the Sudan.

Cities: San Francisco, Alexandria and Seville.

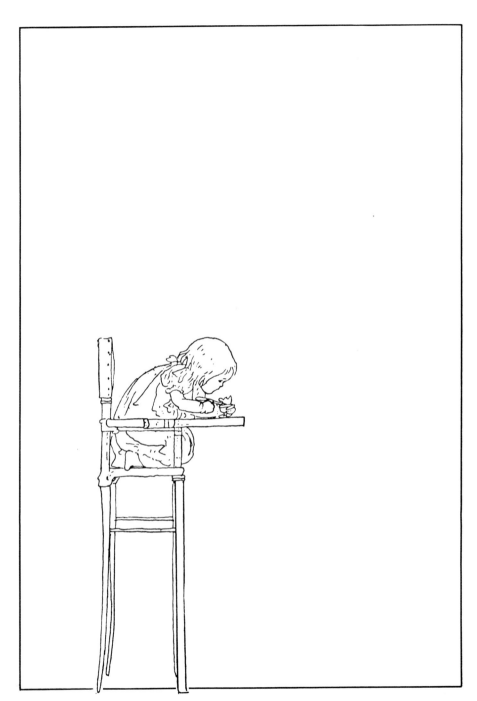

Equipment and clothes

ESSENTIAL EQUIPMENT

There is a great diversity of attractive and expensive baby equipment on the market and before you have experienced caring for a child, the choice can be quite bewildering. If you are limited either for space of for money it is difficult to make sensible decisions. This section is intended to give a guide to what is essential for the comfort of your newborn baby and to give you some tips on how to spend economically.

Remember that it is not necessary to buy all your baby-kit brand new. 'As new' items are available from many sources as babies do not wear out prams, cots or even clothing in their first years. Talk to your friends, look in your local newspaper or insert a 'wanted' ad. yourself and scan round charity shops. Buying second-hand will allow you to be more choosy about the quality of your equipment and this is preferable to buying cheap new items of inferior standard. Obviously some people take better care of their belongings than others, but so much is always available that you can afford to be selective about the people from whom you buy. Having friends prepared to sell you items is ideal as you know the environment from which they have come. You may also have relatives and friends who will loan equipment when their babies have outgrown the initial stages. In some towns, mothers are setting up shops of second-hand baby equipment, and they stress that everything passed to them to sell must be in good condition. It would be worth while finding out if you live near such a shop. Along similar lines, a group of mums near you may have organised an equipment and toy-swapping circle.

When you are preparing for your new baby, think in advance. Do take into account the fact that your baby will develop more quickly than you may expect, and that in no time at all you will be putting things away and wanting new things. If you see advertised a stairgate or a pushchair, or even a high-chair or a playpen, think carefully about whether your particular situation will require one.

If you have a small home or limited finances, only buy essentials. With forethought, a few carefully chosen items will serve the purpose of many.

If you do not like the idea of buying second-hand or borrowing, then do be selective about where you buy from. Have a good look around at all the models available and then compare prices in the different baby-stores. If you can, wait for the sales to see if you can buy items at reduced prices.

Let us, then, provide you with an idea of what we consider to be essential equipment for a baby:

CARRYCOT

A multitude of designs exist, but, before making your choice, think carefully about which features are most important for you in your circumstances. There are two types that are particularly versatile and which you might consider.

The first is a sturdy and stronger-than-average carrycot, together with a chrome transporter that will accommodate a shopping tray. This combines all the features of a pram together with the compactness and adaptability, within the home, of a carrycot. Remember that, although a traditional pram comes apart into the same component parts, the body of the pram is a great deal heavier and more unwieldy and is therefore not suitable for being moved frequently up and down stairs or from room to room.

A sensible alternative might be a pram-buggy. This consists of a lightweight carrycot that fits on to a compact transporter that later will transform into a pushchair. As this is small and light it is ideal if you live in a flat or have stairs to climb. It is also handy if you travel by public transport or intend to take your baby into the shops with you. However, only a limited amount of shopping can be suspended in bags from the handles. Extension handles are available if you are taller than average.

If you decide to buy a more traditional pram, remember that if you are short you should buy a low one giving clear visibility so that you are not putting your baby at risk when you cross roads.

COT

There is no reason why your new baby should not sleep in a cot straight away. However, you may decide to leave this until he is a few months old. When you do buy a cot make sure that the bars are not less than 2¾ inches (6.98 cm) or more than 3½ inches (8.89 cm) apart and that it carries the British Standard Safety No 1753. A sturdy cot with a good mattress is a worthwhile investment. A Vis-i-vent safety mattress, which can also be bought to fit a carrycot, is not cheap but does ensure that your baby can breathe when lying face down, and this will avoid undue anxiety. Dual-height cots save unnecessary bending and awkward postures when putting a sleeping baby down. A dropside can also be an aid. Many cots incorporate a teething rail, which is a plastic cover over the upper horizontal bars.

CHANGING MAT

Most baby stores sell these, all at about the same price, so choose a pattern either to coordinate with your colour scheme or to be attractive to your baby. One of these mats simplifies changing as it prevents soiling towels or the changing surface and it is easy to clean.

EQUIPMENT TIDY

There are many attractive baskets and boxes on the market, or one can easily be made, in which to keep all the cleansing materials you will be using daily for bathing and changing. Essentials to buy include safety pins, tissues or soft toilet tissue and cotton wool. If you find cotton-wool balls easier to use in the first few weeks, unwind a strip from an economy roll, leave it to fluff out over a radiator, then tear it up and make enough little balls to fill a container. Further items you might need are a little bowl for water (such as a pretty margarine tub), baby lotion or oil, a zinc-and-castor-oil mixture or a protective cream for your baby's bottom. A hair brush, sponge, shampoo and soap will also be needed.

Do remember that as your baby becomes more active, these items should be kept well out of his reach.

NAPPY-BUCKET

Choose a pail with a lid and of a size large enough to cope with several nappies in solution. Most commercial nappy-buckets tend to be small and pricey and a beer-making bucket might be more suitable. Two buckets are a good idea — one for soiled nappies and one for wet ones. The latter only need soaking in water before they are washed. Sterilising solution, of which many brands are available at chemists, helps avoid nappy rash; alternatively, if you bottle-feed your baby, you may use the sterilising water from the bottles as this needs to be changed every 24 hours. Household bleach is also perfectly adequate.

DRIERS/AIRERS

Remember that if you are using terry nappies you will need to wash and dry the equivalent of 8 – 12 hand-towels every two days in addition to clothing. In the summer this is usually no problem but in winter you will need extra drying space.

An over-the-bath airer with several rungs is very useful. Alternatively an airer on pulleys that can be lowered from the ceiling could be fitted in a large bathroom, kitchen or utility room. There are also wall-airers that extend across the room and retract when not in use. If you have a tumble-drier, this will overcome the problem entirely.

BATH

A baby-bath usually has only a short life — until your baby begins to kick and slop water everywhere — so you may prefer to make-do with bathing in the sink or a plastic bowl. When he is a few months old he will be large enough to go into the big bath. If you decide to buy a baby-bath you will probably want to buy a non-slip mat. There are tiny ones available but you will find that an adult mat fits most baby baths. This can then be transferred to the big bath and the whole family can benefit from it.

COMFORTABLE CHAIR FOR FEEDING

You do not need to rush out and buy a new chair but — in particular if you are breastfeeding — you will need to be very comfortable. A low chair without arms is recommended, but if you do not have one, then make sure that you are comfortable in whatever you already have. Maybe sitting on the bed will suit you.

STERILISING EQUIPMENT

All bottles, teats and dummies (used by your baby), together with a feeder cup, teaspoon and bowls later on when he is being weaned, need to be regularly sterilised. Kits designed for this purpose are convenient, or a large bowl or 4-litre ice-cream container kept covered is sufficient. Items that float, such as teats, can be submerged in a small jam-jar and larger things held down with a saucer. Sterilising liquid and tablets can be obtained from chemists. Follow the instructions carefully and remember that metal objects are not suitable but china, plastics and glass are.

BOUNCING CRADLE

Your baby will soon start to look around him, and when he is awake will need to be stimulated and not just left lying down. The bouncing cradle gives adequate support to a young baby, who will be able to look around and see what is going on. It is light and easy to move from one room to another, so he can watch what you are doing or be placed in sight of a mobile. Little toys such as rattles can be attached to the strap to keep him amused.

AMUSEMENTS FOR BABY

When your baby is lying down in his room he will prefer to have something to look at rather than blank walls, so bear this in mind when decorating. If you do not choose patterned wallpaper, put up bright tasteful pictures or posters. A good wall-frieze is an idea and will be educational later on, while mobiles fascinate a small baby and are easily made. First toys to consider are those that tiny hands can hold and which make a variety of noises with only slight movement. If you can, take your baby into the shop and shake a few rattles to see which provokes the greatest response. Other suggestions are a sputnik-shaped first ball, a soft toy with slim floppy limbs and a set of colourful stacking beakers, all of which a baby will soon learn to grasp. A floating globe that chimes easily with the movement of the water will help ensure that bathtime is fun.

When buying toys consider colour, shape, sound and texture and try to ensure that your baby has variety.

CLOTHES AND LINEN

Do not buy too many clothes in the first size as your baby will rapidly grow out of them, and if he is particularly big at birth he may never fit in the smallest size at all. Think about your baby's wardrobe well in advance and decide how many knitted items you would like in each size so that you can let any knitting relatives or friends know what would be most useful. If you do not do this you might end up with ten first-size white cardigans for the summer, which would be a great pity. In general, avoid clothing with fiddly fasteners as these are awkward to do up on a wriggly baby. Try to ensure that your baby has natural fibres — that is, cotton and wool — next to the skin.

Everybody's idea of how to dress their child is different, and the seasons of the year and two sexes make it impossible to draw up a definite list of baby clothes. This is just an idea of what you might need.

BEDDING

Sheets and blankets, both carrycot- and cot-size, are needed and both can easily be made from old ones you are not using. If your baby is to begin by sleeping in a carrycot you might not need the smaller carrycot sheets as the larger cot sheets will fold under the mattress perfectly well. Baby-stores sell a variety of bedlinen. Soft blankets such as cellular ones mould better to baby's shape and are easier to use. One single bed-size cellular blanket folds well to fit a cot.

TOWELS

Two large soft towels will be useful. You do not need to buy new towels, but it is a good idea to have at least one special towel set aside just for your baby.

NAPPIES

Two dozen nappies should be enough, but again, do buy good-quality ones, as, although more expensive initially, in the long run they will be longer-lasting. Before buying check with the *Which* magazine surveys, which will give you a guide to the quality of what you are actually buying. Before your baby is born, practise folding nappies so that you are not preoccupied with the mechanics of this at the same time as getting used to your baby's tiny body. In the first few weeks, when your baby is likely to wake for a feed and change several times in the night, a pile of ready-folded nappies can cut down on the time you spend awake. Later on, when your baby is sleeping through the night, you may find the overnight nappy becomes drenched. Two nappies folded together can overcome this problem.

NAPPY LINERS

Nappy liners are placed between bottom and nappy and when soiled can be flushed straight down the toilet. It is worth knowing that if they are only wet and not soiled they can be washed and re-used, provided they are not one-way nappy liners. These one-way liners are more expensive, and only necessary if your baby suffers frequently and badly from a sore bottom.

PLASTIC PANTS

Tie-on plastic pants come in packets of about 6 or 10, and are very good for a new-born baby as they can be adjusted to fit limbs, however tiny, so there is less leakage on to outer clothes. Other types available for the growing baby are elasticated or have studs. If your baby is to wear disposable nappies you will need pants with pockets, which are available either as tie-ons or with studs. Some disposables incorporate both nappy and pants. However, it is a good idea to slip an extra pair of waterproof pants over the top. Duralite pants last a lot longer than plastic ones but are a great deal more expensive.

VESTS

Vests are easier to use if they have an envelope neck, and easier to wash and keep in shape if they are cotton. Button-under vests avoid gaps in clothing around baby's middle and also the droopy nappy look. In summer time a set of pretty cotton T-shirts may be all that you need.

NIGHTDRESSES

There are very pretty nightdresses in cotton which are practical until your baby can move around but you will need bootees and tights as well.

BOOTEES

You will need only a couple of pairs if you normally dress your baby in stretch suits, tights or dungarees with feet in.

STRETCHSUITS

Stretchsuits are ideal for the first few months unless the weather is particularly hot. Make sure you move on to the next size before your baby's toes begin to get squashed.

SLEEPING SUITS

If your baby is a restless sleeper and throws the bedclothes off, sleeping suits either with legs in or as sleeping bags are useful. A dressing gown is not really necessary until he can walk.

CARDIGANS AND JUMPERS

Cardigans for the first few months and jumpers later on are always useful. Acrylic ones are easier to wash than wool and may be more comfortable for your baby to wear. Cardigans that button right up to the neck will keep your baby warmer in winter. If there are a lot of buttons, fasten the lower ones before slipping the garment over the baby's head. When you are making clothes later on remember to add an extra inch or two in length if you have a slim baby. Most patterns are still designed for the plump look!

DRESSES

After the first few months dresses must be short enough for your little girl to crawl without catching her knees. For most of the year you will need tights as well to keep out the draughts. Socks and bootees tend to work their way off an infant's feet until he is old enough to walk properly.

DUNGAREES

Dungarees with a bib both at the front and the back will prevent straps from slipping off your child's shoulders.

SHOES

Avoid shoes until your child is walking confidently. An extra pair of socks or bootees will keep his feet quite warm enough when sitting in the pram or pushchair.

OUTDOOR WEAR

Outdoor wear is very important and there are many items to choose from. *Shawls* are traditional for carrying a tiny baby in but a *carrying cape* is easier to manage. This consists of a roomy cape with a hood that can be quickly put over a baby for visits to neighbours and the short distance between car and front door. *Knitted jackets* with a hood attached fulfil the same need when your child is a little older. They are simpler to use than a cardigan and a bonnet and avoid the chilly draught about the neck.

If you intend to carry your baby in a front sling or, after a few months, in a rucksack you will need a *waterproof suit*. Make sure you buy one that has legs in it and not the sleeping-bag variety. These are also very useful once your child starts sitting in a pushchair. *Sunhats* are just as important in summer as *bonnets* are in winter as a baby rarely has enough hair to protect his delicate skin. If the weather is particularly hot or you are going abroad a sunhat that extends over the shoulders is a worthwhile investment.

Mittens can be attached to each other with elastic or ribbon that goes up the arms of a coat and across the back. This saves losing mittens, which is otherwise almost inevitable as it does not take children long to discover that they can pull them off with their teeth.

CHECKLIST OF FURTHER ITEMS

The following pieces of equipment are not listed under initial equipment but are extremely useful, some especially if you travel around and visit friends or relations a lot.

SAFETY EQUIPMENT FOR YOUR CAR

If you have a car, these are a must to ensure the greatest possible safety for your child in case of an accident, and also to prevent an older child from causing an accident. The tiny baby will travel in a carrycot, and restraints are available that hold the carrycot secure and prevent jolting if you have to brake suddenly. The next progression is to a car seat, and the important thing about this is to ensure that it is fixed properly into your car. Car seats are expensive items but very easy to buy second-hand. Do make sure when you buy one (especially second-hand) that all the straps are with it, as otherwise it may well be useless. Also, make sure that the model you buy will fit into your particular car, as the attachments vary for saloons, estates and hatchbacks. When your child outgrows the car seat he should wear a harness or seat belt.

HIGH-CHAIR

Once your baby can sit up, he can be fed in a high-chair, which will make life a great deal easier for you and more interesting for him. There are two basic types of high-chair.

The first is a multi-purpose frame that converts from a reclining chair to a high-chair. Some of these fold flatter than others, — a point to consider if you need to move it frequently through a doorway. Most of these models have very splayed legs, for stability. This kind can be used in its reclining position when your baby is only a few weeks old.

The second type of high-chair starts life as a high-chair and later converts to a low-chair and table. This is ideal for a single child but may cause problems if you have to take your toddler's 'special' table and chair away for a new baby.

Most high-chairs are big and bulky, and if you are limited in space or travel around a lot you will be interested to learn that there is available a fabric harness, which can be attached to most normal dining chairs, in which your child can be placed and secured. It is basically a flat piece of tough material which anyone who sews could quite easily make. It is very practical, being light, but you should never leave your child alone in one because it is not rigid in any way.

As an alternative, your child can be placed on a chair with a cushion, and secured with a child-harness and anchors. Whichever method you use, make sure that your baby can sit up well before you attempt either.

SLINGS

A sling can be very handy to carry your child around in as it frees both your hands to carry or do other things. Some mothers wear their sling around the house during their normal daily routine, others use it specifically for going on journeys. There are two types — side slings, which require extra support from one arm, and front slings, which are a lot more successful. There are a variety of styles, some of which give additional head support for your baby, so look around, both at the carrying pouch and the straps, before you decide which one will suit you best.

RUCKSACK

To continue in the carrying vein, you may prefer to carry your baby on your back. If so, you will find a child rucksack particularly useful when shopping, or if you are the outdoor type, when walking or going on picnics — in fact, anywhere you may go where a pushchair will be cumbersome. Your baby must be able to support himself to a certain extent before you put him in one of these, unlike the sling, which a newborn baby can go straight into. You should get a lot of use out of it, as even a large toddler will enjoy being carried on your back and will fit into the rucksack. The more modern ones have a stand, which makes the loading and unloading of your child easier, but you must never leave him alone in it as it could easily topple.

PUSHCHAIR

When buying your pushchair, think carefully about when you will use it, as they vary tremendously in build and weight. Probably the most popular pushchairs today are the buggies, which are light and handy for travelling and convenient for shopping. The lie-back buggy has all the advantages of a buggy and is also quite suitable for a tiny baby to sleep in. A further advantage to using a buggy is that if you have a second child, you can buy an attachment for a second buggy so that you can push two together. This combination is convenient as they separate easily; however, the two together are very wide, which may be awkward in shops. An alternative is to have a second seat welded on, and this will take less space sideways. As some buggies convert from prams to pushchairs, this may well be the best answer for you if you have a baby and a toddler.

Another useful pushchair if you have two small children is the tandem pushchair, which is the width of a normal pushchair but longer, as the children sit one in front of the other, the back seat reclining for when baby is tiny. This is heavier than the buggy but does fold flat, so it can be transported by car. When both children are sitting-up the shopping tray underneath can be used, which is an added advantage as buggies will only take a small amount of shopping before becoming unstable.

The more conventional pushchair is stronger than the buggy, but its only real advantages are that it can carry more shopping and it moves better over uneven ground.

You can buy hoods and canopies to attach to all the different kinds of pushchairs. You will need to buy reins or a harness to fasten your child securely into a pushchair whatever the model.

PRAM SEAT

A pram seat should only be fitted on to a proper pram, as a carrycot used as a pram is not stable enough to support a seat and child. Again, your toddler will need to be strapped into the seat so that he does not fall out. And beware if he is a wriggler, as he may cause the pram to sway and fall over. It is not really advisable to leave your toddler sitting in the seat while you go into shops.

SAFETY-GATE

Once your baby is crawling around and learning to stand and walk, you will probably find that you need a safety-gate. If you have stairs, it will be essential, until you have taught your child the correct way to climb up and down them. Even if you live in a flat or bungalow you may find one useful to place in a doorway or passageway, to keep your child either in or out of a certain area. Most leading baby-shops sell them. Some are expanding, others standard, so check on the widths you will need before you buy one. If you use your safety-gate properly you will probably find that a playpen is unnecessary.

Safety-gates are very popular second-hand items, so if you get the opportunity to buy one before you need it, go ahead and get it, as otherwise you may find one hard to come by when you most need it.

Registration
of birth and
christening

REGISTRATION OF BIRTH

Most parents have spent quite a long time before their child is born choosing a name or names for the new arrival. Some, however, still have to decide after their baby is born. It is therefore important to know that by law your child must be officially registered within 42 days (6 weeks) of his birth.

Many maternity hospitals today have either a resident registrar or one who visits regularly, probably several times a week. You can find out his hours and place of business from the Ward Sister. If your stay in hospital is short and does not coincide with the visits of the registrar, then either you or your husband may return any time within the 42 days to register your child. If your confinement is at home, your midwife or the local Town Hall will be able to advise you on where to go for the registration. This may be either the nearest maternity hospital or a registry office.

The details the registrar will request are the full names of both partners, your dates and places of birth, place and date of your marriage, your husband's occupation and your present address. Also, the place and date of birth, names and sex of your baby. If you are not married and both partners wish to declare their parenthood you will both have to attend the registration.

There are two versions of the birth certificate. One is short and precise, stating only the baby's name, sex, date and place of birth, and this is free. You can, however, buy a copy of the more elaborate certificate, which includes details of both parents as well as of the child.

CHRISTENING YOUR CHILD

To many people the christening or baptism of their child is automatic a few months after the baby is born, and they may look upon it as a family celebration in which their child is named.

In fact the baptism ceremony has nothing to do with the official naming of a child or adult. It is, rather, an important occasion in which a person commits himself to his faith, and shows his willingness to join the Christian community and way of life, and so it is not uncommon for an adult to be baptised.

In the case of a small child or baby, the Church will baptise and welcome him into the congregation on the assurance that the child will receive a Christian upbringing. This is why both the parents and the godparents or the congregation promise to ensure that the child is encouraged to attend Church or Meetings and Sunday School. They also promise to set a good example to the child at home and in the community by their own prayers and Christian actions. Adults accept the responsibility for this as a baby is too young to understand and accept the significance of his baptism.

If parents would like their child baptised in a parish other than their own, the vicars of both churches need to be consulted and give their approval before the ceremony can take place. Details of the ceremony vary from one denomination to another but your vicar will remind you of these beforehand. The majority of churches do, however, now issue and recognise a common Certificate of Baptism.

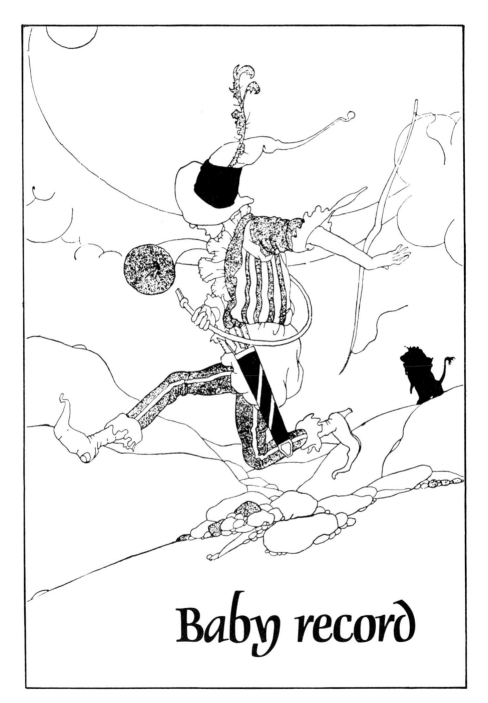

Baby record

ARRIVAL

_____

_____

was born at _____ hours

on _____

at _____

Weight _____

Length _____

Colour of hair _____

Colour of eyes _____

Midwife _____

Birth announcement

GROWTH

Age	Height	Weight

IMMUNIZATIONS RECORD

Dates

	1st	2nd	3rd	booster
Diphtheria				
	1st	2nd	3rd	booster
Tetanus				
	1st	2nd	3rd	booster
Poliomyelitis				
	1st	2nd	3rd	booster

Whooping cough ⎯⎯⎯⎯⎯⎯⎯⎯⎯⎯⎯⎯⎯⎯⎯⎯⎯

Measles ⎯⎯⎯⎯⎯⎯⎯⎯⎯⎯⎯⎯⎯⎯⎯⎯⎯⎯⎯⎯⎯

Tuberculosis ⎯⎯⎯⎯⎯⎯⎯⎯⎯⎯⎯⎯⎯⎯⎯⎯⎯⎯⎯

German measles (girls only) ⎯⎯⎯⎯⎯⎯⎯⎯⎯⎯⎯⎯

Other vaccinations (e.g. for foreign travel) ⎯⎯⎯⎯⎯⎯

RECORD OF CHILDHOOD ILLNESSES

Chicken pox —————————————————————

Measles —————————————————————————

Mumps —————————————————————————

German measles ————————————————————

Whooping cough ———————————————————

Scarlet fever ————————————————————————

Others ————————————————————————

—————————————————————————————

—————————————————————————————

—————————————————————————

—————————————————————————

——————————————————————

——————————————————

————————————————

—————————————

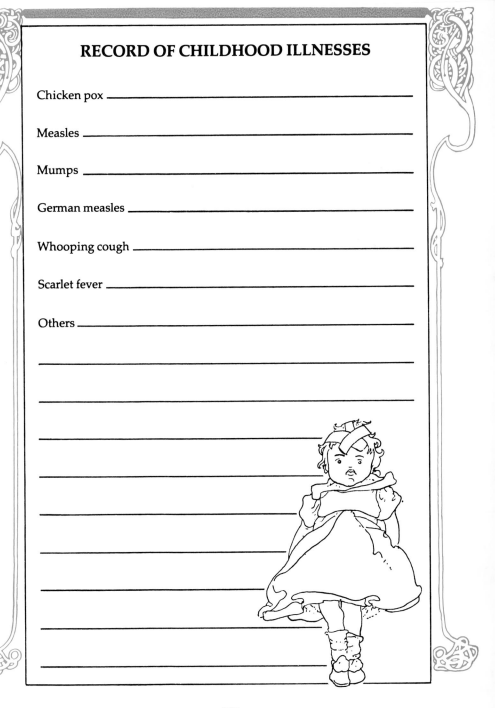

ARRIVAL

_____

_____

was born at _____ hours

on _____

at _____

Weight _____

Length _____

Colour of hair _____

Colour of eyes _____

Midwife _____

Birth announcement

GROWTH

Age	Height	Weight

IMMUNIZATIONS RECORD

Dates

	1st	2nd	3rd	booster
Diphtheria				
Tetanus				
Poliomyelitis				

Whooping cough _____

Measles _____

Tuberculosis _____

German measles (girls only) _____

Other vaccinations (e.g. for foreign travel) _____

_____

_____

_____

_____

_____

_____

_____